RabbitMQ Essentials

Hop straight into developing your own messaging
applications by learning how to utilize RabbitMQ

David Dossot

BIRMINGHAM - MUMBAI

RabbitMQ Essentials

Copyright © 2014 Packt Publishing

First published: April 2014

Production Reference: 1180414

Published by Packt Publishing Ltd.
Livery Place
35 Livery Street
Birmingham B3 2PB, UK.

ISBN 978-1-78398-320-9

www.packtpub.com

Credits

Author
David Dossot

Reviewers
Ken Pratt
Ken Taylor
Ignacio Colomina Torregrosa
Héctor Veiga

Commissioning Editor
Ashwin Nair

Acquisition Editor
Richard Harvey

Content Development Editor
Govindan K

Technical Editors
Shruti Rawool
Nachiket Vartak

Copy Editors
Aditya Nair
Kirti Pai

Project Coordinator
Puja Shukla

Proofreader
Ameesha Green

Indexer
Monica Ajmera Mehta

Graphics
Sheetal Aute
Ronak Dhruv
Abhinash Sahu

Production Coordinator
Alwin Roy

Cover Work
Alwin Roy

Cover Image
Sheetal Aute

Foreword

What gets me most excited about RabbitMQ is that people keep finding new and better ways to use it. Messaging has truly come of age and stands beside databases and web applications as a technology that every professional developer needs to know.

In 2006, when RabbitMQ was born, messaging was mostly used by companies that had way too many IT systems and desperately needed some way to connect them. Jargon words such as "pubsub" and "queue" were strictly for messaging geeks and highly paid integration consultants. But the world was already changing and we were about to find out why.

Today's software and web applications are increasing in scale rapidly. There are more users, apps, devices, places, and ways to connect; this creates a burning need to build more scalable applications. At the same time, these new applications have to integrate with existing systems and services written using any language or API you care to think of. There is only one way to deliver scalability in this kind of environment: use messaging. The best way to do that is via a product such as RabbitMQ.

We started RabbitMQ because there was no messaging tool that was really powerful and dependable, yet easy to get started with. We decided to make one. We hope you like it.

The fun part is designing the tool so that you, the developer, feel like RabbitMQ is actually helping you to build better apps, instead of getting in the way. Your use of the tool should grow with your system.

The hard part is balancing simplicity and power. With RabbitMQ, we think we got this about right. Developers have little tolerance for complexity and nonsense. But beware! There is such a thing as "fake simplicity"; if a tool makes promises that seem too good to be true, then something is almost certainly broken. A truly simple system makes its capabilities obvious when they are needed. RabbitMQ will never lie to you or conceal its true behavior and we think this is essential in a good tool.

In this book, David Dossot has shown how messaging can help anyone architect and design solid scalable apps and how RabbitMQ can deliver on this promise. In 2014, everyone can grok the basics of messaging. Read this book to get started.

Alexis Richardson
Former CEO, Rabbit Technologies Inc.

About the Author

David Dossot has worked as a software engineer and an architect for more than 18 years. He has been using RabbitMQ since 2009 in a variety of different contexts. He is the main contributor to the AMQP transport for Mule. His focus is on building distributed and scalable server-side applications for the JVM and the Erlang VM. He is a member of IEEE, the Computer Society, and AOPA, and holds a diploma in Production Systems Engineering from ESSTIN.

He is a co-author for the first and second editions of *Mule in Action* (*Manning Publications Co.*). He is a Mule champion and a DZone Most Valuable Blogger. He commits on multiple open source projects and likes to help people on Stack Overflow. He's also a judge for the annual Jolt Awards software competition.

I would like to thank my wife for giving the thumbs up to this book project, while just recovering from the previous book. It was a stretch goal, but with her support and the patience and love of the rest of my family, it became possible. I'm also grateful to the rainy winters we get in the Pacific Northwest as I didn't feel bad staying inside writing!

I would like to extend a special thanks to our early reviewers — without them, the book wouldn't be as great as it is now. I want to use this opportunity to give kudos to a bunch of first class software engineers and architects who have inspired me and from whom I've learned so much throughout my career: Romuald van der Raaij, André Weber, Philip Thomas, Pierre-Antoine Grégoire, Carl Schmidt, Tim Meighen, Josh Devins, Dominic Farr, Erik Garrett, and Ken Pratt.

About the Reviewers

Ken Pratt has over 10 years of professional experience in software development, and knows more programming languages than you can imagine. He has shipped multiple products powered by RabbitMQ and enjoys discovering new ways to structure systems.

Ken Taylor has worked in software development and technology for over 15 years. During the course of his career, he has worked as a systems analyst on multiple software projects in several industries as well as U.S. government agencies. He has successfully used RabbitMQ for messaging on multiple projects. He previously reviewed *RabbitMQ Cookbook*, written by *Sigismondo Boschi* and *Gabriele Santomaggio, Packt Publishing*. He is a member and speaker of the 757 Ruby users group and the Hampton Roads .NET Users Group (HRNUG). He holds an A.S. degree in Computer Science from the Paul D. Camp Community College and was awarded a U.S. patent for a real estate financial software product. He is currently working at Outsite Networks Inc. in Norfolk, Virginia. He lives in Suffolk, Virginia with his lovely wife, Lucia, and his two sons, Kaide and Wyatt.

> I would like to thank my wife for her support while writing this book, and my sons for reminding me the importance of being inquisitive. I would also like to thank Packt Publishing for asking me to participate as a technical reviewer in this excellent resource on RabbitMQ.

Ignacio Colomina Torregrosa is a technical engineer in Telecommunications and has a master's degree in Free Software. He works as a PHP/Symfony developer and he has experience using RabbitMQ as a tool to optimize and improve the performance of web applications that deal with a large amount of traffic.

Héctor Veiga is a software engineer specializing in real-time data integration. Recently, he has focused his work on different cloud technologies such as AWS, Heroku, OpenShift, and so on to develop scalable, resilient, and high-performing applications to handle high-volume real-time data in diverse protocols and formats. Additionally, he has a strong foundation in messaging systems knowledge such as RabbitMQ and AMQP. Also, he has a master's degree in Telecommunications Engineering from the Universidad Politécnica de Madrid and a master's degree in Information Technology and Management from the Illinois Institute of Technology.

He currently works at HERE as a part of Global Data Integrations and is actively developing scalable applications to consume data from several different sources. HERE heavily utilizes RabbitMQ to address their messaging requirements. In the past, he worked at Xaptum Technologies, a company dedicated to M2M technologies. He has also reviewed *RabbitMQ Cookbook* written by *Sigismondo Boschi* and *Gabriele Santomaggio, Packt Publishing*.

I would like to thank my family and friends for their support. Specially, I would like to acknowledge my family in Chicago: David, Pedro, Javier, Jorge, Daniela, Gerardo, and Jaime; without them, this would not have been possible.

www.PacktPub.com

Support files, eBooks, discount offers and more

You might want to visit www.PacktPub.com for support files and downloads related to your book.

Did you know that Packt offers eBook versions of every book published, with PDF and ePub files available? You can upgrade to the eBook version at www.PacktPub.com and as a print book customer, you are entitled to a discount on the eBook copy. Get in touch with us at service@packtpub.com for more details.

At www.PacktPub.com, you can also read a collection of free technical articles, sign up for a range of free newsletters and receive exclusive discounts and offers on Packt books and eBooks.

http://PacktLib.PacktPub.com

Do you need instant solutions to your IT questions? PacktLib is Packt's online digital book library. Here, you can access, read and search across Packt's entire library of books.

Why Subscribe?

- Fully searchable across every book published by Packt
- Copy and paste, print and bookmark content
- On demand and accessible via web browser

Free Access for Packt account holders

If you have an account with Packt at www.PacktPub.com, you can use this to access PacktLib today and view nine entirely free books. Simply use your login credentials for immediate access.

Table of Contents

Preface

RabbitMQ is an open source messaging broker that implements the AMQP protocol. In the past few years, its popularity has been growing. Initially used by the most daring companies, many are now discovering not only RabbitMQ's particular virtues, but also the positive impact of using messaging in software engineering. Indeed, with the advent of cloud computing, the need to architect and build systems that both scale and degrade gracefully has become more pressing. Opting for loosely coupled architectures, tied together by a message passing through brokers such as RabbitMQ, software engineers have been able to satisfy the needs of modern application development.

RabbitMQ Essentials takes the readers through the journey of Clever Coney Media, a fictitious company with real-world problems. Starting with their first step of RabbitMQ, we will follow the company as they develop their understanding and usage of messaging across their different applications. From one-way asynchronous message passing to request-response interactions, the reader will discover the wide range of applications that messaging with RabbitMQ enables.

This book covers the core principles of the AMQP protocol and best practices for its usage. It also details some of the proprietary extensions that RabbitMQ has added to the protocol and why and when it makes sense to use them. The interoperability of AMQP is demonstrated throughout the book, with examples written in different programming languages.

This book will teach readers all they need to not only get started with their projects, but also grow them, through gaining a deep and wide understanding of the capacities of RabbitMQ and AMQP. The code has a prominent place in this book, with an accent put on the detailed production-grade examples.

What this book covers

Chapter 1, A Rabbit Springs to Life, introduces the reader to the notion of messaging and its benefits. After introducing AMQP and RabbitMQ, the reader will learn how to install and configure RabbitMQ, and get ready to start developing applications with it.

Chapter 2, Creating an Application Inbox, discusses the usage of RabbitMQ to create a simple message inbox. By the end of this chapter, you'll know how to connect to RabbitMQ and publish direct and topic exchanges and get messages out of queues.

Chapter 3, Switching to Server-push, describes a more efficient way to consume messages and route them to end users. It also introduces the fanout exchange and teaches you how it can be used to reach many queues while publishing only a single message.

Chapter 4, Handling Application Logs, keeps building on the previously learned concepts and puts them in action in the context of aggregating application usage data. You'll also learn about the notion of quality of service and how it can be used to improve performance. You'll perform a load test of your RabbitMQ application.

Chapter 5, Tweaking Message Delivery, discusses the usage of RabbitMQ extensions for the AMQP protocol to make undelivered messages expire and deal with them when this happens. It also discusses the standard options that can be used to ensure the success of message deliveries.

Chapter 6, Smart Message Routing, explains how the headers' exchange can be used to perform a property-based routing of messages and how request-response styles of interactions can be achieved with RabbitMQ.

Chapter 7, Taking RabbitMQ to Production, presents different strategies that can be used to deal with the potential failures of the RabbitMQ broker. In this context, you'll learn about clustering and federation. You'll also read about monitoring RabbitMQ to ensure a smooth production ride.

Chapter 8, Testing and Tracing Applications, describes the challenges that are inherent to distributed systems and what mitigation strategies can be used to alleviate them.

Appendix, Message Schemas, lists all the schemas used to specify the JSON representation of the messages in the different examples.

What you need for this book

Readers with a good command of Java and some knowledge of Ruby and Python will feel the most at ease when reading the code samples. Thus, readers with C, C++, and C# experience should be able to make the most of the Java samples. Finally, the discussion around code samples will benefit all readers, especially those with an exposure to the middleware software engineering.

We will install and configure RabbitMQ as part of the first chapter, so you do not need to worry about this. However, you will need the following software installed before running the code examples:

- **JDK 7 and Maven 3 to run the Java examples**: The former can be downloaded from `http://www.oracle.com/technetwork/java/javase/downloads/jdk7-downloads-1880260.html` and the latter from `http://maven.apache.org/download.cgi`.

- **Ruby 2.0 (or equivalent JRuby) and Bundler to run the Ruby examples**: Ruby can be downloaded from `https://www.ruby-lang.org/en/downloads/`. The installation of Bundler is detailed at `http://bundler.io/#getting-started`.

- **Python 2.7 to run the Python examples**: This can be downloaded from `http://www.python.org/download/` and to manage dependencies, you can download the pip package from `http://www.pip-installer.org`.

- **PHP 5.3 to run the PHP examples**: This can be downloaded from `http://www.php.net/downloads.php`.

- **Apache JMeter and the AMQP plugin to run load tests**: These can be downloaded from `http://jmeter.apache.org/download_jmeter.cgi` and `https://github.com/jlavallee/JMeter-Rabbit-AMQP`, respectively.

Who this book is for

This book discusses architectural and programming concepts in the context of messaging; as such, it addresses a wide audience from software architects to engineers. It focuses on building applications with RabbitMQ using different popular programming languages and therefore, contains lot of code. No prior experience with message-oriented middleware is required.

Conventions

In this book, you will find a number of styles of text that distinguish between different kinds of information. Here are some examples of these styles, and an explanation of their meaning.

Code words in text, database table names, folder names, filenames, file extensions, pathnames, dummy URLs, user input, and Twitter handles are shown as follows: "The first of these additions takes care of declaring the topic exchange in the existing onApplicationStart method."

A block of code is set as follows:

```
rabbitMqManager.call(new ChannelCallable<DeclareOk>()
{
    @Override
    public String getDescription()
    {
        return "Declaring topic exchange: " + USER_TOPICS_EXCHANGE;
    }
```

When we wish to draw your attention to a particular part of a code block, the relevant lines or items are set in bold:

```
try
{
    connection = factory.newConnection();
    connection.addShutdownListener(this);
    LOGGER.info("Connected to " + factory.getHost() + ":" +
        factory.getPort());
}
```

Any command-line input or output is written as follows:

```
$ sudo service rabbitmq-server restart
```

New terms and **important words** are shown in bold. Words that you see on the screen, in menus or dialog boxes for example, appear in the text like this: "When connected to the management console, click on the **Exchanges** tab."

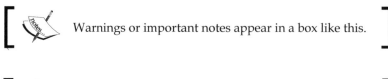

Warnings or important notes appear in a box like this.

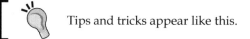

Tips and tricks appear like this.

Reader feedback

Feedback from our readers is always welcome. Let us know what you think about this book—what you liked or may have disliked. Reader feedback is important for us to develop titles that you really get the most out of.

To send us general feedback, simply send an e-mail to feedback@packtpub.com, and mention the book title through the subject of your message.

If there is a book that you need and would like to see us publish, please send us a note in the SUGGEST A TITLE form on www.packtpub.com or e-mail suggest@packtpub.com.

If there is a topic that you have expertise in and you are interested in either writing or contributing to a book, see our author guide on www.packtpub.com/authors.

Customer support

Now that you are the proud owner of a Packt book, we have a number of things to help you to get the most from your purchase.

Downloading the example code

You can download the example code files for all Packt books you have purchased from your account at http://www.packtpub.com. If you purchased this book elsewhere, you can visit http://www.packtpub.com/support and register to have the files e-mailed directly to you.

Errata

Although we have taken every care to ensure the accuracy of our content, mistakes do happen. If you find a mistake in one of our books—maybe a mistake in the text or the code—we would be grateful if you would report this to us. By doing so, you can save other readers from frustration and help us improve subsequent versions of this book. If you find any errata, please report them by visiting http://www.packtpub.com/support, selecting your book, clicking on the **errata submission form** link, and entering the details of your errata. Once your errata are verified, your submission will be accepted and the errata will be uploaded to our website, or added to any list of existing errata, under the Errata section of that title.

Piracy

Piracy of copyright material on the Internet is an ongoing problem across all media. At Packt, we take the protection of our copyright and licenses very seriously. If you come across any illegal copies of our works, in any form, on the Internet, please provide us with the location address or website name immediately so that we can pursue a remedy.

Please contact us at copyright@packtpub.com with a link to the suspected pirated material.

We appreciate your help in protecting our authors, and our ability to bring you valuable content.

Questions

You can contact us at questions@packtpub.com if you are having a problem with any aspect of the book, and we will do our best to address it.

1
A Rabbit Springs to Life

Messaging or message queuing is a style of communication between applications or components that enables a loosely coupled architecture. **Advanced Message Queuing Protocol (AMQP)** is a specification that defines the semantics of an interoperable messaging protocol. RabbitMQ is an Erlang-based implementation of AMQP, which supports advanced features such as clustering.

In this chapter, we will cover the following topics:

- Introducing concepts and terminology related to messaging
- Discovering AMQP and RabbitMQ
- Presenting the context in which all the book's examples will take place
- Installing and configuring RabbitMQ

What is messaging?

Smoke signals, couriers, carrier pigeons, and semaphores: if this was a riddle, you would think of messages right away. Humanity has always had the need to connect with each other, finding new ways to defy the challenge posed by the distance between the different groups of people who need to communicate. We've come a long way with modern technologies, but essentially the basics remain. Senders, recipients, and messages are the core of all our communication infrastructures.

Software applications have the same needs; systems need to exchange messages with each other. They sometimes need to be sure that the message sent has reached its destination. They sometimes need to receive an immediate response, but not all the time. In some cases, they may even need to receive more than one response. Based on these different needs, different styles of communication between systems have emerged.

All this can be explained with the help of the following figure:

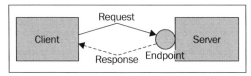

The request-response style of interaction

This request-response style of interaction is the most common style; a system (acting as a client) interacts with a remote system (acting as a server) via a synchronous interaction with a remotely exposed communication endpoint. Whether it takes the form of a remote procedure call, a web service invocation, or consumption of a resource, the model is the same: one system sends a message to another and waits for the remote party to respond synchronously. Systems communicate with each other in a point-to-point manner.

The advantages of this approach are met with inconveniences. On one hand, programmers get a simple programming model as everything happens in a procedural fashion. On the other hand, the tight coupling between both parties has a deep impact on the architecture of the whole system as it is hard to evolve, hard to scale, and so on.

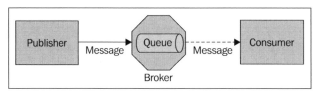

One-way interaction with message queuing

Enter the one-way style of interaction, where systems interact with each other in an asynchronous fashion via the transmission of messages, and generally through the intermediary of relaying parties known as message brokers. In this scheme, commonly referred to as messaging or message queuing, systems play the role of message publishers (producers) and message consumers. They publish a message to a broker on which they rely on to deliver it to the intended consumer. If a response is required, it will eventually come at some point on time through the same mechanism, but reversed (the consumer and producer roles will be swapped).

A loosely coupled architecture

The advantage of the messaging approach is that systems are loosely coupled. They don't need to know exactly where they are located; a mere name is enough to reach them. Systems can, therefore, be evolved in an independent manner with no impact on each other as the reliability of message delivery is entrusted to a broker. This is demonstrated in the following figure:

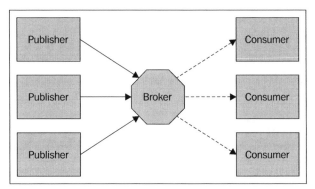

Message enabling a loosely coupled architecture

Indeed, the architecture represented in the preceding figure allows the following:

- The publishers or consumers fail without impacting each other
- The performance of each side to leave the other side unaffected
- The number of instances of publishers and consumers to grow and reduce and to accommodate their workload in complete independence
- The publishers are unaware of the location and technology of the consumers and vice-versa

The main downside of this approach is that programmers cannot rely on the mental model of procedural programming where things immediately happen one after another. In messaging, things happen over time, so systems must be programmed to deal with it.

If all this is a little blurry, let's use an analogy of a well-known protocol: **Simple Mail Transfer Protocol (SMTP)**. In this protocol, e-mails are published (sent) to an SMTP server. This initial server then stores and forwards the e-mail to the next SMTP server, and so on until the recipient e-mail server is reached. At this point, the message is queued in an inbox, waiting to be picked up by the consumer (typically, via POP3 or IMAP). With SMTP, the publisher has no idea when the e-mail will be delivered or whether it will eventually be delivered at all. In case of a delivery failure, the publisher can be notified of issues later down the line. The only sure fact is that the broker has successfully accepted the message it had initially sent.

Furthermore, if a response is needed, it will arrive asynchronously using the same delivery mechanism but with the publisher and consumer roles reversed. The entire process is demonstrated in the following figure:

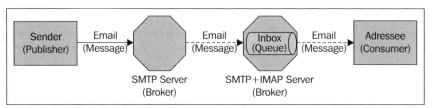

The e-mail infrastructure as an analogy for message queuing

With these fundamental notions established, let's now delve into the messaging protocol that we are going to consider in this book: **Advanced Message Queuing Protocol (AMQP)**.

Meet AMQP

The **Advanced Message Queuing Protocol (AMQP)** is an open standard that defines a protocol for systems to exchange messages. AMQP defines not only the interaction that happens between a consumer/producer and a broker, but also the over-the-wire representation of the messages and commands that are being exchanged. Since it specifies the wire format for messages, AMQP is truly interoperable—nothing is left to the interpretation of a particular vendor or hosting platform. And since it is open, the AMQP community has flourished with broker and client implementations in a wide range of languages.

The AMQP 0-9-1 specification can be downloaded at http://www.rabbitmq.com/resources/specs/amqp0-9-1.pdf.

Let's look at the following list of core concepts of AMQP, which we will revisit in detail in the upcoming chapters:

- **Broker**: This is a middleware application that can receive messages produced by publishers and deliver them to consumers or to another broker.

- **Virtual host**: This is a virtual division in a broker that allows the segregation of publishers, consumers, and all the AMQP constructs they depend upon, usually for security reasons (such as multitenancy).

- **Connection**: This is a physical network (TCP) connection between a publisher/consumer and a broker. The connection only closes on client disconnection or in the case of a network or broker failure.

- **Channel**: This is a logical connection between a publisher/consumer and a broker. Multiple channels can be established within a single connection. Channels allow the isolation of the interaction between a particular client and broker so that they don't interfere with each other. This happens without opening costly individual TCP connections. A channel can close when a protocol error occurs.

- **Exchange**: This is the initial destination for all published messages and the entity in charge of applying routing rules for these messages to reach their destinations. Routing rules include the following: direct (point-to-point), topic (publish-subscribe) and fanout (multicast).

- **Queue**: This is the final destination for messages ready to be consumed. A single message can be copied and can reach multiple queues if the exchange's routing rule says so.

- **Binding**: This is a virtual connection between an exchange and a queue that enables messages to flow from the former to the latter. A routing key can be associated with a binding in relation to the exchange routing rule.

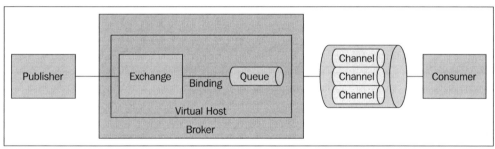

Overview of the concepts defined by the AMQP specification

You may have a message-queuing background and are by now wondering what are the main differences between AMQP and another protocol that you know. Here is a quick comparison of some of the main features:

- **Java Message Service (JMS)**: Unlike AMQP, this only defines the wire protocol for a Java programming interface and not messages. As such, JMS is not interoperable and only works when compatible clients and brokers are used. Moreover, unlike AMQP, it does not define the commands necessary to completely configure messaging routes, leaving too much room for vendor-specific approaches. Finally, in JMS, message producers target a particular destination (queue or topic), meaning the clients need to know about the target topology. In AMQP, the routing logic is encapsulated in exchanges, sparing the publishers from this knowledge.

- **MQ Telemetry Transport (MQTT)**: This is an extremely lightweight message-queuing protocol. MQTT focuses only on the publish-subscribe model. Like AMQP, it is interoperable and is very well suited for massive deployments in embedded systems. Like AMQP, it relies on a broker for subscription management and message routing. RabbitMQ can speak the MQTT protocol—thanks to an extension.

- **ØMQ (also known as ZeroMQ)**: This offers messaging semantics without the need for a centralized broker (but without the persistence and delivery guarantees that a broker provides). At its core, it is an interoperable networking library. Implemented in many languages, it's a tool of choice for the construction of high-performance and highly-available distributed systems.

- **Process inboxes**: Programming languages and platforms such as Erlang or Akka offer messaging semantics too. They rely on a clustering technology to distribute messages between processes or actors. Since they are embedded in the hosting applications, they are not designed for interoperability.

Multiple commercial and open source implementations of AMQP are available. Often, existing messaging brokers have been extended with an AMQP adapter, like in the case of ActiveMQ.

The open source broker we will look at in detail for this book has been built from the ground to support AMQP. So let's now turn our focus on RabbitMQ.

The RabbitMQ broker

RabbitMQ is an Erlang implementation of an AMQP broker. Erlang has been chosen to build it because of its intrinsic support for building highly-reliable and distributed applications. Indeed, it is used to run telecommunication switches for which a proverbial total system's availability of 9 nines has been reported (that's 32 milliseconds of downtime per year). Erlang is also able to run on any operating system.

RabbitMQ implements Version 0-9-1 of AMQP with custom extensions (as allowed by the protocol) and some undeprecations (for features RabbitMQ really wants to keep). For data persistence, it relies on Mnesia, the in-memory/file-persisted embedded database of Erlang, and specific message storage and index files. For clustering, it mainly relies on Erlang's ingrained clustering abilities. RabbitMQ can easily be extended with the addition of plugins; for example, a web-based administration console can be deployed on it, thanks to this mechanism. This is shown in the following diagram:

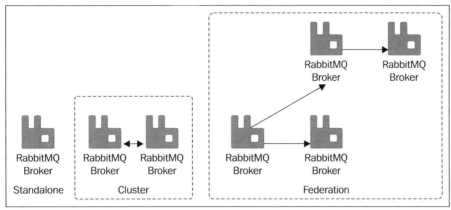

The RabbitMQ broker engaging in various topologies

As shown in the preceding figure, RabbitMQ brokers can not only be clustered together, they can also be connected together using different techniques, such as federation and shovels, in order to form messaging topologies with smart message routing across brokers and the capacity to span multiple data centers.

What's the deal with AMQP 1.0?

AMQP 1.0 was published at the end of 2011 after the development and maintenance of AMQP was transferred to OASIS. Why hasn't RabbitMQ rushed to support this version, since it seems to be the first official release? The fact of the matter is that AMQP has been drastically revised between 0-9-1 and 1.0. It was so drastic that some core concepts, such as the exchange, no longer exist. So, AMQP 1.0 is a different protocol than 0-9-1, with no truly compelling reason to adopt it. It is not more capable than 0-9-1, and some would also argue that it has lost some of the key aspects that made it attractive in the first place.

We're done with our quick introduction to messaging, AMQP, and RabbitMQ. In the next section, we will introduce Clever Coney Media, a fictitious company that just discovered RabbitMQ and will put it to service for the greater good!

A case for RabbitMQ

Clever Coney Media (CCM) is a fictitious integrated software and digital media agency that specializes in developing applications for online communities. Their software landscape, as shown in the following figure, is a hodgepodge of technologies:

- Its flagship product is a **Rich Internet Application (RIA)**, backed by a Java backend. It's used by end users to engage in thematic online communities.

- The back office is built with Ruby on Rails.

- The company's website and blog runs on PHP.

- A bunch of ad hoc Python scripts are used to extract and message data in order to generate usage reports.

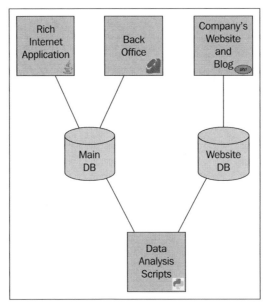

Clever Coney Media's heterogeneous software landscape

You may wonder, why is CCM looking at adding RabbitMQ to their already busy environment? The main driver for this is a new feature it wants to offer to their users, which is the capacity to send messages to other users. Think of it as a mix of chat, without the immediateness, and e-mail, without the long-running history. Instead of creating its own messaging infrastructure, it's decided to use a ready-made message oriented middleware like RabbitMQ.

We'll see in the rest of the book that as its knowledge and usage of RabbitMQ increases, CCM will discover new opportunities to leverage it in its environment. But for now, enough with the ado; let's follow CCM as it gets started with its very first step with RabbitMQ.

Getting RabbitMQ ready

To get started, we will go through the following three installation and configuration steps:

- Installing the RabbitMQ broker
- Installing the management plugin
- Configuring the vhost and user

Installing the broker

CCM runs its production servers on Ubuntu Linux. Most of the developers' workstations run Mac OS X and Linux, while some run Windows. This heterogeneity is not a concern for RabbitMQ, which can run natively on all these operating systems.

RabbitMQ provides complete online installation guides for all the supported operating systems (you can access these at http://www.rabbitmq.com/download.html). In our case, we will follow the instructions for Debian/Ubuntu.

For greater control, we do not wish to use the RabbitMQ APT repository; instead, we want to download the Debian package and manually install it, as follows:

```
$ wget http://www.rabbitmq.com/releases/rabbitmq-server/v3.2.1/rabbitmq-server_3.2.1-1_all.deb
$ sudo dpkg -i rabbitmq-server_3.2.1-1_all.deb
$ sudo apt-get -f --force-yes --yes install
```

> **Downloading the example code**
>
> You can download the example code files for all Packt books you have purchased from your account at http://www.packtpub.com. If you purchased this book elsewhere, you can visit http://www.packtpub.com/support and register to have the files e-mailed directly to you.

In case you wonder why we first ran the dkpg software followed by the apt-get command, the reason is simple: the first attempt expectedly fails because none of the Erlang dependencies are present in our system. This failure generates a list of unresolved dependencies that the apt-get command picks up and installs, including the installation of the RabbitMQ broker.

The installation of RabbitMQ has also installed Erlang on your machine. Though not absolutely required for using RabbitMQ, we want to encourage you to discover this simple yet powerful language and platform. You can learn more about Erlang at http://www.erlang.org/. You can also consider Elixir as an alternative language for the Erlang VM at http://elixir-lang.org.

We can verify that the RabbitMQ broker is actually working using the standard service command:

```
$ sudo service rabbitmq-server status
Status of node 'rabbit@ip-172-31-31-18' ...
[{pid,4027},
 {running_applications,[{rabbit,"RabbitMQ","3.2.1"},
                        {mnesia,"MNESIA  CXC 138 12","4.5"},
                        {os_mon,"CPO  CXC 138 46","2.2.7"},
                        {xmerl,"XML parser","1.2.10"},
                        {sasl,"SASL  CXC 138 11","2.1.10"},
                        {stdlib,"ERTS  CXC 138 10","1.17.5"},
                        {kernel,"ERTS  CXC 138 10","2.14.5"}]},
 {os,{unix,linux}},
 {erlang_version,"Erlang R14B04 (erts-5.8.5) [source] [64-bit] [rq:1]
[async-threads:30] [kernel-poll:true]\n"},
 {memory,[{total,27085496},
          {connection_procs,2648},
          {queue_procs,5296},
          {plugins,0},
          {other_proc,9040296},
          {mnesia,57776},
          {mgmt_db,0},
          {msg_index,25768},
          {other_ets,752416},
          {binary,1952},
          {code,14546600},
          {atom,1360921},
          {other_system,1291823}]},
 {vm_memory_high_watermark,0.4},
```

```
{vm_memory_limit,247537664},
{disk_free_limit,50000000},
{disk_free,7020503040},
{file_descriptors,[{total_limit,924},
                   {total_used,3},
                   {sockets_limit,829},
                   {sockets_used,1}]},
{processes,[{limit,1048576},{used,122}]},
{run_queue,0},
{uptime,73}]
...done.
```

If you're wondering what format is used to represent the server status information, it's not JSON but in fact, Erlang lists and tuples. You can notice how the status data contains a lot of contextual information about RabbitMQ and the Erlang VM.

> The default folders where the package has installed files are `/etc/rabbitmq` for configuration files, `/usr/lib/rabbitmq` for application files, and `/var/lib/rabbitmq` for data files.

If you take a look at the running processes for RabbitMQ, you'll find both the service wrapper and the Erlang virtual machine (also known as BEAM) running as follows:

```
$ pgrep -fl rabbitmq

3633 /bin/sh /usr/sbin/rabbitmq-server

3647 /usr/lib/erlang/erts-5.8.5/bin/beam.smp -W w -K true -A30 -P
1048576 -- -root /usr/lib/erlang -progname erl -- -home /var/lib/
rabbitmq -- -pa /usr/lib/rabbitmq/lib/rabbitmq_server-3.1.5/sbin/../ebin
-noshell -noinput -s rabbit boot -sname rabbit@pegasus -boot start_sasl
-config /etc/rabbitmq/rabbitmq -kernel inet_default_connect_options
[{nodelay,true}] -sasl errlog_type error -sasl sasl_error_logger false
-rabbit error_logger {file,"/var/log/rabbitmq/rabbit@pegasus.log"}
-rabbit sasl_error_logger {file,"/var/log/rabbitmq/rabbit@pegasus-sasl.
log"} -rabbit enabled_plugins_file "/etc/rabbitmq/enabled_plugins"
-rabbit plugins_dir "/usr/lib/rabbitmq/lib/rabbitmq_server-3.1.5/sbin/../
plugins" -rabbit plugins_expand_dir "/var/lib/rabbitmq/mnesia/rabbit@
pegasus-plugins-expand" -os_mon start_cpu_sup false -os_mon start_disksup
false -os_mon start_memsup false -mnesia dir "/var/lib/rabbitmq/mnesia/
rabbit@pegasus"
```

You may find that when RabbitMQ runs, a process named epmd is also running. This is the Erlang Port Mapper Daemon in charge of coordinating Erlang nodes in a cluster. It is expected to start even if you are not running clustered RabbitMQ.

Note that by default, the broker service is configured to auto-start when the Linux host starts. You can confirm and configure this via a tool called rcconf as shown in the following screenshot:

```
rcconf - Debian Runlevel Configuration tool

    [*] apparmor                   AppArmor initialization
    [*] grub-common                Record successful boot for GRUB
    [*] landscape-client           Landscape client daemons
    [*] ondemand                   Set the CPU Frequency Scaling governor to "ondemand"
    [*] pppd-dns                   Restore resolv.conf if the system crashed.
    [*] rabbitmq-server            Enable AMQP service provided by RabbitMQ broker
    [*] rsync                      fast remote file copy program daemon
    [*] sudo                       Provide limited super user privileges to specific users
    [ ] acpid
    [ ] apport
    [ ] atd
    [ ] console-setup
```

The RabbitMQ server service auto-starts by default

Installing the management plugin

By default, RabbitMQ does not embed a web-based management console but offers it as an optional plugin. This management console makes it very easy to peek into a running RabbitMQ instance, so we definitely want to have it installed from the get go.

The Debian package has installed several scripts, one of them being `rabbitmq-plugins`, whose purpose is to allow the installation and removal of plugins. Let's use it to install the management plugin as follows:

```
$ sudo rabbitmq-plugins enable rabbitmq_management
The following plugins have been enabled:
  mochiweb
  webmachine
  rabbitmq_web_dispatch
  amqp_client
  rabbitmq_management_agent
  rabbitmq_management
Plugin configuration has changed. Restart RabbitMQ for changes to take effect.
```

Yes, it is that easy! As invited by the installer, we need to restart RabbitMQ as follows:

```
$ sudo service rabbitmq-server restart
* Restarting message broker rabbitmq-server          [ OK ]
```

Using our favorite web browser, we can now reach the home page of the management console by navigating to `http://<hostname>:15672` as shown in the following screenshot:

The login screen of the management console

So, what **Username** and **Password** can we use to log in to the console? None yet, but we're going to to have a remedy for that too!

Configuring users

One of the scripts installed by the Debian package is `rabbitmqctl`, which is the RabbitMQ broker control script. It is of paramount importance as it is used to configure all aspects of the broker. We will now use it to configure an administration user in the broker as follows:

```
$ sudo rabbitmqctl add_user ccm-admin hare123
Creating user "ccm-admin" ...
...done.


$ sudo rabbitmqctl set_user_tags ccm-admin administrator
Setting tags for user "ccm-admin" to [administrator] ...
...done.
```

By default, RabbitMQ comes with a guest user authenticated with the guest password. You'll want to change this password to something else as follows:

```
sudo rabbitmqctl change_password guest guest123
```

By navigating back to the management console login screen, we are now able to log in with `ccm-admin` and `hare123`. We are welcomed by this overview of the broker's internals, as shown in the following screenshot:

The main dashboard of the management console

Note that at this point, the `ccm-admin` user is not able to introspect any exchange or queue in any virtual host. We will address this issue in a moment. But for now, we need another user for development purposes so that our applications can connect to RabbitMQ. So, let's create the `ccm-dev` user as follows:

```
$ sudo rabbitmqctl add_user ccm-dev coney123
Creating user "ccm-dev" ...
..done.
```

As discussed earlier in this chapter, RabbitMQ supports the notion of **virtual hosts**, which are logical subdivisions of its execution space. We're going to create a virtual host, also known as **vhost**, for the development environment. So, anything that happens in it happens in isolation from any other environments we can create in the future (such as a QA environment). So, let's create a vhost named `ccm-dev-vhost` as follows:

```
$ sudo rabbitmqctl add_vhost ccm-dev-vhost
Creating vhost "ccm-dev-vhost" ...
..done.
```

> RabbitMQ comes with a default vhost named / on which the guest user has full permissions. Though this is convenient for quick tests, we recommend that you create dedicated vhosts in order to keep concerns separated so that it is possible to completely drop a vhost and restart from scratch without unexpected impacts.

As it currently is, neither the `ccm-admin` nor `ccm-dev` users have permission to do anything on `ccm-dev-vhost`. Let's fix this by giving the vhost full rights on it as follows:

```
$ sudo rabbitmqctl set_permissions -p ccm-dev-vhost ccm-admin ".*" ".*"
".*"
Setting permissions for user "ccm-admin" in vhost "ccm-dev-vhost"
...done.


$ sudo rabbitmqctl set_permissions -p ccm-dev-vhost ccm-dev ".*" ".*"
".*"
Setting permissions for user "ccm-dev" in vhost "ccm-dev-vhost"
...done.
```

What have we just done? Most of the command is straightforward but the `".*" ".*" ".*"` part looks a tad mysterious, so let's analyze it. It is a triplet of permissions for the considered vhost that respectively grant configure, write, and read permissions on the designated resources for the considered user and vhost. Resources, which consist of exchanges and queues, are designated by regular expressions that match their names. Thus, in our case, we are allowing any resource via the `.*` regular expression.

The actual commands that are granted depend on the resource type and the granted permissions. The reader can get a complete list of the access control policies supported by RabbitMQ at `http://www.rabbitmq.com/access-control.html`.

As an alternative to all command lines, you can also turn to the user management features of the management console. If you click on the **Admin** tab of the console and then on the **ccm-dev** user listed in the **Users** tab, you'll see what's shown in the following screenshot. The entire user configuration you've set from the command line is visible and editable in the management console.

Details of an individual user in the management console

Summary

A lot of ground was covered in this chapter. We learned about the architectural and design promises of messaging and how AMQP and RabbitMQ deliver on these promises. We discovered the reason why Clever Coney Media decided to introduce RabbitMQ in their software landscape. Finally, we installed and configured a RabbitMQ broker.

It's time to hit the ground running and write some code. You can now turn to the next chapter to start building your first RabbitMQ-powered application!

2
Creating an Application Inbox

Applications that need to use RabbitMQ need to establish a permanent connection to it. When this connection is established, logical channels can be created and message-oriented interactions, such as publishing and getting messages, can be performed. After learning these fundamentals, you'll learn how exchange-routing strategies determine how messages are delivered to queues. In particular, you will learn about direct exchange, which delivers messages to a single queue, and topic exchange, which delivers messages to multiple queues based on pattern-matching routing keys.

In this chapter, we will discuss the following topics:

- Establishing a solid connection to RabbitMQ

- Working with channels

- Publishing messages to RabbitMQ

- Getting messages from RabbitMQ

- Direct and topic exchanges

Connecting to RabbitMQ

Before delving into the code, let's quickly summarize what **Clever Coney Media (CCM)** wants to achieve with RabbitMQ. As said in the previous chapter, it wants to add an application inbox to allow users of its web application to send messages to each other. The expected user experience is more like that of an e-mail than instant messaging, though messages will be transient by definition; once received, it will not be possible to read it again. Thus, message queuing is a perfect match for it; each user will have a dedicated message queue where messages will wait until retrieval.

The following diagram illustrates the architecture CCM has in place and where RabbitMQ will fit in:

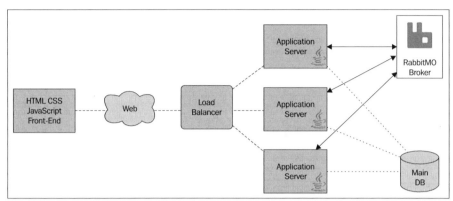

CCM's main application architecture

From what you've learned in *Chapter 1, A Rabbit Springs to Life*, you need to establish a physical (network) connection between the application servers and RabbitMQ, which will multiplex many logical channels. Unlike creating channels, creating connections is a costly operation, very much like it is with database connections. Typically, database connections are pooled, where each instance of the pool is used by a single execution thread. AMQP is different in the sense that a single connection can be used by many threads through many multiplexed channels. Thus, establishing a single long-lived connection between each application server and RabbitMQ should be enough to support the needs of this new feature, until it's proven that it gets saturated by traffic and multiple connections become a necessity.

So for now, CCM will start with a single connection. Since the **Rich Internet Application** is written in Java, we will discover this client API first. According to the documentation, connecting to RabbitMQ is as simple as the following:

```
ConnectionFactory factory = new ConnectionFactory();
factory.setUsername(userName);
factory.setPassword(password);
factory.setVirtualHost(virtualHost);
factory.setHost(hostName);
factory.setPort(portNumber);
Connection connection = factory.newConnection();
```

This seems easy enough, but CCM is worried about writing production-grade code, that is, code that can gracefully handle failures. What if RabbitMQ is not running? Clearly, it does not want to take their whole application down if this happens. What if RabbitMQ needs a restart? They also want their application to recover gracefully when that occurs. In fact, they want their application to keep functioning whether the whole messaging subsystem is working or not. The user experience will be altered accordingly.

In summary, the behavior CCM aims at is the following:

- The application should start whether a connection to RabbitMQ can be established or not
- If the connection to RabbitMQ is lost, it should reconnect by itself
- If the connection is down, sending or fetching messages should fail gracefully

> There are ready-made libraries that wrap the RabbitMQ client and make all this possible, such as **Spring AMQP** (`http://projects.spring.io/spring-amqp`), **Mule AMQP** (`http://www.mulesoft.org/connectors/amqp-connector`), or **Beetle** (`https://github.com/xing/beetle`). CCM wants to learn the basics and underlying mechanisms for itself and so do we; hence, we will not use any of them in this book. Consider using them in your projects.

Let's now detail the implementation of the `RabbitMqManager` class created to reify this behavior. You will discover it piece by piece and comment it as you go, as follows:

```java
public class RabbitMqManager implements ShutdownListener
{
    private final static Logger LOGGER =
      Logger.getLogger(RabbitMqManager.class.getName());

    private final ConnectionFactory factory;
    private final ScheduledExecutorService executor;
    private volatile Connection connection;

    public RabbitMqManager(final ConnectionFactory factory)
    {
        this.factory = factory;
        executor = Executors.newSingleThreadScheduledExecutor();
        connection = null;
    }
```

The goal of the `RabbitMqManager` class is to babysit a single connection to RabbitMQ. Therefore, it keeps a single reference to a `Connection` instance with a `null` value, meaning it is not connected. Because reconnection attempts will be made asynchronously, in order to avoid mobilizing a thread of the main application, an executor is created to be able to run asynchronous tasks. The `Connection` variable is declared `volatile` so that it is visible to all threads at all time.

This manager attempts connecting only when its `start` method is called, so let's now look into the following code:

```java
public void start()
{
    try
    {
        connection = factory.newConnection();
        connection.addShutdownListener(this);
        LOGGER.info("Connected to " + factory.getHost() + ":" +
            factory.getPort());
    }
    catch (final Exception e)
    {
        LOGGER.log(Level.SEVERE, "Failed to connect to " +
            factory.getHost() + ":" + factory.getPort(), e);
        asyncWaitAndReconnect();
    }
}
```

What's notable about this code is that it registers the `RabbitMqManager` class itself as a listener for connection shutdown events so that its `shutdownCompleted` method (which we'll discuss in a moment) is called when something bad happens to the connection. It also deals with a connection failure on start by calling `asyncWaitAndReconnect`, a method that we'll look at right now in the following code:

```java
private void asyncWaitAndReconnect()
{
    executor.schedule(new Runnable()
    {
        @Override
        public void run()
        {
            start();
        }
    }, 15, TimeUnit.SECONDS);
}
```

As you can see, this method simply schedules a restart of the whole `RabbitMqManager` class to happen in 15 seconds. Why the wait? The main reason is that you want to avoid thrashing on reconnection attempts; there's no point in retrying a reconnection too fast. In fact, a simple exponential back-off strategy could easily be bolted on this code. Let's now look at the following method called by the RabbitMQ Java client when something goes sour with the connection:

```java
@Override
public void shutdownCompleted(final ShutdownSignalException cause)
{
    // reconnect only on unexpected errors
    if (!cause.isInitiatedByApplication())
    {
        LOGGER.log(Level.SEVERE, "Lost connection to " +
            factory.getHost() + ":" + factory.getPort(),
                cause);

        connection = null;
        asyncWaitAndReconnect();
    }
}
```

The important aspects here are that we only try a reconnection if the connection shutdown was not initiated by the application, which happens on a normal application termination, and that we reconnect asynchronously in order to avoid mobilizing the RabbitMQ client thread that called the `shutdownCompleted` method. What's left to look at is the `stop` method that's used to cleanly terminate `RabbitMqManager` as follows:

```java
public void stop()
{
    executor.shutdownNow();

    if (connection == null)
    {
        return;
    }

    try
    {
        connection.close();
    }
    catch (final Exception e)
    {
```

```
            LOGGER.log(Level.SEVERE, "Failed to close connection", e);
        }
        finally
        {
            connection = null;
        }
    }
}
```

Again, nothing complex here. After issuing a termination of the executor in charge of running the reconnection attempts, the connection itself is cleanly disposed of; all this in the context of Java's verbose but mandatory exception-handling mechanism. With this in place, connecting to RabbitMQ still looks very much like the example from the documentation, but now with robustness mixed in as follows:

```
ConnectionFactory factory = new ConnectionFactory();
factory.setUsername("ccm-dev");
factory.setPassword("coney123");
factory.setVirtualHost("ccm-dev-vhost");
factory.setHost("localhost");
factory.setPort(5672);

RabbitMqManager connectionManager = new RabbitMqManager(factory);
connectionManager.start();
```

Establishing a connection is the basis for doing anything with RabbitMQ; however, the real work happens in channels. Let's see what CCM came up with in that matter.

Working with channels

The `Channel` instances are created by the `Connection` object; therefore, the logical location to place the channel creation logic is in `RabbitMqManager`, as follows:

```
public Channel createChannel()
{
    try
    {
        return connection == null ? null : connection.createChannel();
    }
    catch (final Exception e)
    {
        LOGGER.log(Level.SEVERE, "Failed to create channel", e);
        return null;
    }
}
```

Again, this is quite simple; if anything goes awry when creating a channel, the method returns `null`. This is in line with what CCM desires, to shield the application from any RabbitMQ-related failures. Instead of dealing with exceptions coming from the messaging subsystem, it will just have to deal with potential `null` values. In the same spirit, the disposal of channels is delegated to a method that takes care of potential exceptions as follows:

```
public void closeChannel(final Channel channel)
{
    // isOpen is not fully trustable!
    if ((channel == null) || (!channel.isOpen()))
    {
        return;
    }

    try
    {
        channel.close();
    }
    catch (final Exception e)
    {
        LOGGER.log(Level.SEVERE, "Failed to close channel: " +
            channel, e);
    }
}
```

Note that the `isOpen` method can't be fully trusted; another thread may close the channel after this check is done. So, the call to the `close` method could still fail because the channel might have closed already.

 Though channel instances are technically thread safe, it is strongly recommended that you avoid having several threads using the same channel concurrently.

Realizing that the "open channel, do something with the channel, close channel" scenario may occur regularly in the code, CCM decides to support it by creating some code artifacts. It first creates an interface that defines what the contract for this pattern should be, as follows:

```
public interface ChannelCallable<T>
{
    String getDescription();

    T call(Channel channel) throws IOException;
}
```

Then, it adds a method to `RabbitMqManager` in order to execute such a `ChannelCallable` instance, as follows:

```
public <T> T call(final ChannelCallable<T> callable)
{
    final Channel channel = createChannel();

    if (channel != null)
    {
        try
        {
            return callable.call(channel);
        }
        catch (final Exception e)
        {
            LOGGER.log(Level.SEVERE, "Failed to run: " +
                callable.getDescription() + " on channel: " +
                channel, e);
        }
        finally
        {
            closeChannel(channel);
        }
    }

    return null;
}
```

Again, the invoker of this `call` method will be shielded from any error that could stem from the messaging layer; it will just receive `null` if something goes wrong. Notice how the `ChannelCallable` description is used in the log message. The guiding principle here is that you should always provide as much contextual information as possible when something goes wrong.

CCM is quite happy with its core infrastructure code. It is now able to connect to a RabbitMQ broker, open a channel, and issue a series of commands, all in a thread-safe and exception-safe manner. It's now time to build on this foundation!

Building the inbox

If you remember the discussion about AMQP in *Chapter 1, A Rabbit Springs to Life*, messages are published to exchanges from where they get routed to queues, ready to be consumed. A routing strategy determines which queue (or queues) the message will be routed to. The routing strategy bases its decision on a **routing key** (a free-form string) and potentially on message meta-information. In the case of the user-to-user messaging system considered here, one message needs to be routed to the queue acting as the inbox of the addressee. Therefore, the exchange-routing strategy that needs to be used is the **direct** one, which matches the destination queue name with the routing key used when the message is produced, as illustrated in the following figure:

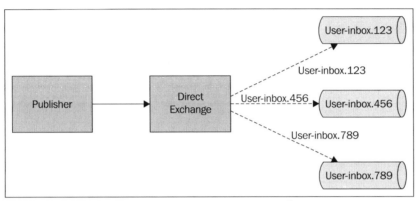

The direct exchange route messages to specific queues

To tie the messaging logic in its application, CCM will piggyback an existing polling mechanism that's already in place between the JavaScript frontend and the Java backend. This is not the most efficient approach, and in fact it will be reviewed as you'll soon find out, but it's the easiest way for it to get started and roll out the feature in the best time frame. The following figure shows how the frontend poll will be used to fetch messages from the user's inbox and a regular AJAX call will be used to send a new message. Messages themselves will be represented as JSON objects (refer to *Appendix, Message Schemas*, for the formal specification of these JSON messages).

They will contain meta-information such as timestamp, sender, and receiver IDs on top of the text contents of the message itself, as shown in the following diagram:

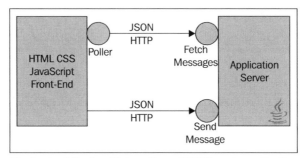

The frontend/backend interactions of CCM's main application

Let's follow the code CCM has created to roll this feature out and learn about the different concepts at the same time. It's created a `UserMessageManager` class to encapsulate all the operations related to this particular feature:

```java
public class UserMessageManager
{
    static final String USER_INBOXES_EXCHANGE = "user-inboxes";

    @Inject
    RabbitMqManager rabbitMqManager;

    public void onApplicationStart()
    {
        rabbitMqManager.call(new ChannelCallable<DeclareOk>()
        {
            @Override
            public String getDescription()
            {
                return "Declaring direct exchange: " +
                    USER_INBOXES_EXCHANGE;
            }

            @Override
            public DeclareOk call(final Channel channel)
              throws IOException
            {
                String exchange = USER_INBOXES_EXCHANGE;
```

```
String type = "direct";
// survive a server restart
boolean durable = true;
// keep it even if nobody is using it
boolean autoDelete = false;
// no special arguments
Map<String, Object> arguments = null;

return channel.exchangeDeclare(exchange, type,
    durable, autoDelete, arguments);
        }
    });
}
```

After receiving the `RabbitMqManager` instance via the dependency injection, it's created an `onApplicationStart` method that, as its name suggests, gets called every time the application server starts. All this method does is declare the exchange where the user-to-user messages are published to. Why do we do this on start? This is because it's a fundamental requirement of the user-to-user messaging subsystem; if the exchange doesn't exist, attempts to publish messages to it will raise exceptions.

Channels are killed by exceptions — in our case, sending to a nonexistent exchange would not only raise an exception, it will also terminate the channel where the error occurred. Any subsequent code that tries to use the terminated channel will fail too. Thus, do not be surprised to see cascades of failures when something goes wrong.

Notice that the method to create the exchange is called declare not create — this is to suggest that if the exchange already exists, it will do nothing; otherwise, it will actually create it. This is why it's safe to declare this every time the application starts. Also, it would be an overkill to do it when every message is sent, so the application start is the best time to do it.

Besides using the **direct** type, we also configure the **durable, autoDelete,** and **arguments** properties of the exchange. We do not want this exchange to go away after a restart of RabbitMQ, nor when it's not being used anymore; hence, the values we've used.

An exchange declaration is idempotent only if the exchange properties are the same. Trying to declare an already existing exchange with different properties will fail. Always use consistent properties in your exchange declaration. If you need to change the properties, you'll need to delete the exchange before declaring it with the new properties. The same rule applies to a queue declaration.

After creating the exchange, the next thing we want to do is to have the user inbox queue created and bound to the exchange. The following is how we do it:

```java
public void onUserLogin(final long userId)
{
    final String queue = getUserInboxQueue(userId);

    rabbitMqManager.call(new ChannelCallable<BindOk>()
    {
        @Override
        public String getDescription()
        {
            return "Declaring user queue: " + queue + ",
              binding it to exchange: "
                    + USER_INBOXES_EXCHANGE;
        }

        @Override
        public BindOk call(final Channel channel)
          throws IOException
        {
            return declareUserMessageQueue(queue, channel);
        }
    });
}

private BindOk declareUserMessageQueue(final String queue,
  final Channel channel) throws IOException
{
    // survive a server restart
    boolean durable = true;
    // keep the queue
    boolean autoDelete = false;
    // can be consumed by another connection
    boolean exclusive = false;
    // no special arguments
    Map<String, Object> arguments = null;
    channel.queueDeclare(queue, durable, exclusive,
      autoDelete, arguments);

    // bind the addressee's queue to the direct exchange
    String routingKey = queue;
    return channel.queueBind(queue, USER_INBOXES_EXCHANGE,
      routingKey);
}
```

Every time a user logs in on the system, the application calls `onUserLogin`. After getting the addressee's queue name from `getUserInboxQueue` (merely `"user-inbox." + userId`), it then calls `declareUserMessageQueue` (you'll soon understand why the method is split in half). In this method, the queue is declared with an approach that's really similar to how it's done for an exchange, but with slightly different properties, as follows:

- `durable`: This is true because you want the queue to stay declared even after a broker restart

- `autoDelete`: This is false because you want to keep the queue even if it's not being consumed anymore

- `exclusive`: This is false because you want this queue to be consumable by other connections (remember we have several application servers connected to RabbitMQ; hence, the queue will be accessed from different connections)

- `arguments`: This is null because you don't need to custom configure the queue

Then the queue is bound to the exchange using its own name as the routing key so that the direct routing strategy can route messages to it. When this is done, publishing messages to the `user-inboxes` exchange will actually deliver messages to the user queue whose name matches the published routing key.

> If no queue is bound to an exchange or if the routing strategy can't find a matching destination queue, the message published to the exchange will be discarded silently. It's possible to optionally be notified when unroutable messages are discarded, as we will see in subsequent chapters.

Again, when the same properties are used, these operations are idempotent, so we can safely declare the queue and bind it to the exchange again and again, each time a user logs in.

Sending user messages

Now let's look at the method of `UserMessageManager` that's in charge of sending messages:

```
static final String MESSAGE_CONTENT_TYPE = "application/vnd.ccm.pmsg.
v1+json";
static final String MESSAGE_ENCODING = "UTF-8";

public String sendUserMessage(final long userId,
  final String jsonMessage)
```

```
{
    return rabbitMqManager.call(new ChannelCallable<String>()
    {
        @Override
        public String getDescription()
        {
            return "Sending message to user: " + userId;
        }

        @Override
        public String call(final Channel channel)
          throws IOException
        {
            String queue = getUserInboxQueue(userId);

            // it may not exist so declare it
            declareUserMessageQueue(queue, channel);

            String messageId = UUID.randomUUID().toString();

            BasicProperties props = new BasicProperties.Builder()
                .contentType(MESSAGE_CONTENT_TYPE)
                .contentEncoding(MESSAGE_ENCODING)
                .messageId(messageId)
                .deliveryMode(2)
                .build();

            String routingKey = queue;

            // publish the message to the direct exchange
            channel.basicPublish(USER_INBOXES_EXCHANGE,
              routingKey, props,
                jsonMessage.getBytes(MESSAGE_ENCODING));

            return messageId;
        }
    });
}
```

Now, you should understand why the `declareUserMessageQueue` method was extracted from `onUserLogin:`. We are calling it in `sendUserMessage` every time one user sends a message to another. Why on earth are we doing that? Haven't we already declared and bound the user queue on login? Well, maybe and maybe not; there is no guarantee that the addressee has ever logged into the system, so as far as the sender is concerned, it's impossible to be sure the destination queue exists. Thus, the safest path is to declare it on every message sent, bearing in mind that this declare operation is idempotent, so it will not do anything if the queue already exists. It may seem strange at first, but it's the sender's responsibility to ensure the addressee's queue exists if they want to be sure the message will not be lost.

> This is a common pattern with AMQP; when there is no strong *happens before* relationship between events, idempotent re-declaration is the way to go. Conversely, the *check, then act* pattern is discouraged; trying to check the pre-existence of an exchange or a queue can't give any guarantee of success in the typical distributed environment where AMQP is used.

The method for publishing a message is very simple. You call `basicPublish` towards the `user-inboxes` exchange, using the queue name as the routing key (as per the **direct** routing), some optional message properties, and an array of bytes that represent the actual message payload. Let's detail the message properties we've associated with the message as follows:

- **contentType**: Because a message is published, thus consumed as a byte array, nothing really says what these bytes represent. Sure, in our current situation, both publishers and consumers are in the same system, in the same class too, so you could implicitly assume the content type is what we expect. This said, the reason we always specify a content type is that we want messages to be self-contained; whichever system ends up receiving or introspecting a message will know for sure what the byte array it contains represents. Moreover, by embedding a version number in the content type (`application/vnd.ccm.pmsg.v1+json`), we future-proof the system in case we later decide to alter the JSON representation of messages.

- **contentEncoding**: You use a specific encoding (UTF-8) when you serialize string messages into byte arrays so that they can be published. Again, in order for the messages to be self-explicit, we provide all the necessary meta-information to allow reading them.

- **messageID**: As you will see later in the book, message identifiers are an important aspect of traceability in messaging and distributed applications. For now, let us just say that you want each message to have a unique identifier, hence the usage of a **UUID** for generating such an identifier.

- **deliveryMode**: This is probably the most mysterious parameter as it is set to 2. The AMQP specification defines the value for this property as follows: for Non-persistent it is set to 1 and for Persistent it is set to 2. Now it's clearer! Indeed, you want a guarantee that the RabbitMQ broker will write the message to the disk so that it won't be lost, no matter what.

> Do not confuse exchange and queue durability with message persistence; non-persistent messages stored in a durable queue will be gone after a broker restart, leaving you with an empty queue.

But what would happen if the sending of the user message fails for example, if the connection with RabbitMQ is broken? In that case, the sendUserMessage class will return null and it will be up to the caller to deal with the issue. In your case, you will simply inform the end user that the messaging application is currently experiencing issues.

> Why would you ever use a non-persistent delivery mode? Isn't the whole point of a message broker such as RabbitMQ to guarantee that messages aren't lost? This is true, but there are circumstances where this guarantee can be relaxed. Consider a scenario where a fire hose-like publisher bombards the broker with a deluge of noncritical messages. In that case, using a non-persistent delivery would spare accessing the host machine's disk, resulting in elevated performances.

Before going any further, let's take a look at the structure of an AMQP message.

AMQP message structure

The following figure illustrates the structure of an AMQP message where you will recognize the four properties we've just used and discover a few more. Note that this figure uses the specification name of the fields; each language implementation renames them slightly so they can be valid names, for example, content-type becomes contentType in Java.

Structure of an AMQP message

Except the reserved one, all these properties are free to use and, unless otherwise specified, are ignored by the AMQP broker. In the case of RabbitMQ, the only field that is supported by the broker is the `user-id` field, which is validated to ensure it matches the name of the broker user that established the connection to the broker. Notice how the `headers` property allows you to add extra key-value pairs in case none of the standard properties fit your needs.

Fetching user messages

We can now turn our attention to the method in `UserMessageManager` that's in charge of retrieving messages. Remember that you're piggybacking a poll request that the frontend regularly sends to the application; therefore, you will retrieve the messages from the user inbox queue in a synchronous manner, holding the application thread in charge of dealing with the poll requests until you've removed all the pending messages from the queue. The channel method to use for this is called `basicGet`. Let's see it in action as follows:

```java
public List<String> fetchUserMessages(final long userId)
{
    return rabbitMqManager.call(new ChannelCallable<List<String>>()
    {
        @Override
        public String getDescription()
        {
            return "Fetching messages for user: " + userId;
        }
        @Override
        public List<String> call(final Channel channel)
```

```
        throws IOException
    {
        List<String> messages = new ArrayList<>();

        String queue = getUserInboxQueue(userId);
        boolean autoAck = true;

        GetResponse getResponse;

        while ((getResponse = channel.basicGet
          (queue, autoAck)) != null)
        {
            final String contentEncoding =
              getResponse.getProps().getContentEncoding();
            messages.add(new String
              (getResponse.getBody(), contentEncoding));
        }

        return messages;
    }
  });
}
```

In the preceding method, you can assume that the user queue exists, and thus, that you can safely get messages from it. This is a reasonable assumption as this method will always be called after onUserLogin has been called for the user, leading to the pre-existence of the queue. Notice how basicGet is called repeatedly until a null response is received, which means the queue is empty. Notice also how you use the content encoding from the received message properties to build a string out of the body's byte array.

One thing remains unclear: what is this autoAck flag about? AMQP brokers rely on client-side acknowledgement for the certainty that a message has been correctly received and can now be permanently destroyed from the broker storage. It is therefore up to the consumer to acknowledge a message if and only if it is done with processing, or if they are certain that there is no risk of losing it if it processes asynchronously. In our case, since the risk of losing a message is acceptable, you do not manually acknowledge messages. Instead, you inform the broker to consider them as acknowledged as soon as we get them (you'll look into manual acknowledgement further in the book).

And that is it! You now have a working user inbox ready to be tested. Sure, it is not extremely fast (we rely on polls) and is wasteful in resources (a channel is created and closed on each poll). However, all in all it works, it doesn't leak resources, and it can recover gracefully from a RabbitMQ broker restart. Let's take a look at the management console when running the application with a dozen simulated users.

Seeing it run

With the application running on a pair of servers connected to RabbitMQ, you can see the following established connections from the management console:

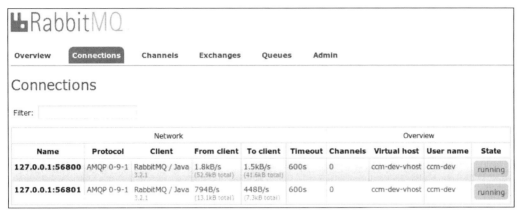

The management console provides connection information

As expected, one connection per application server has been established. Notice how the upstream and downstream network throughputs are clearly represented. What about channels? Because they get opened and closed very quickly, it's actually hard to see any from the management console. With our current architecture, they just don't stay long enough to be rendered on the user interface of the console. So let's look at the following exchanges:

The user-inbox direct exchange shows up in the management console

You can see the user exchange and the rate of messages coming in and out of it. Their being consumed as fast as they come in is a good sign as it means the current architecture is sufficient for our needs and messages are not piling up. However, what are all these other exchanges that we can see here? Clearly, we haven't created them by code, so they should be coming from somewhere. Indeed, the nameless exchange represented as **(AMQP default)** and all the exchanges whose names start with **amq.** are defined by the AMQP specification and, as such, must be provided by default by RabbitMQ. Now, what about queues? Let's have a look at them:

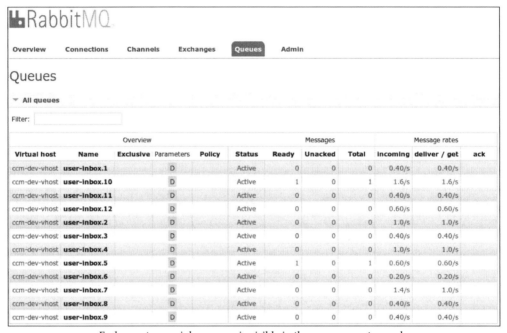

									Message rates		
		Overview					Messages				
Virtual host	Name	Exclusive	Parameters	Policy	Status	Ready	Unacked	Total	incoming	deliver / get	ack
ccm-dev-vhost	user-inbox.1		D		Active	0	0	0	0.40/s	0.40/s	
ccm-dev-vhost	user-inbox.10		D		Active	1	0	1	1.6/s	1.6/s	
ccm-dev-vhost	user-inbox.11		D		Active	0	0	0	0.40/s	0.40/s	
ccm-dev-vhost	user-inbox.12		D		Active	0	0	0	0.60/s	0.60/s	
ccm-dev-vhost	user-inbox.2		D		Active	0	0	0	1.0/s	1.0/s	
ccm-dev-vhost	user-inbox.3		D		Active	0	0	0	0.40/s	0.40/s	
ccm-dev-vhost	user-inbox.4		D		Active	0	0	0	1.0/s	1.0/s	
ccm-dev-vhost	user-inbox.5		D		Active	1	0	1	0.60/s	0.60/s	
ccm-dev-vhost	user-inbox.6		D		Active	0	0	0	0.20/s	0.20/s	
ccm-dev-vhost	user-inbox.7		D		Active	0	0	0	1.4/s	1.0/s	
ccm-dev-vhost	user-inbox.8		D		Active	0	0	0	0.40/s	0.40/s	
ccm-dev-vhost	user-inbox.9		D		Active	0	0	0	0.40/s	0.40/s	

Each user-to-user inbox queue is visible in the management console

As expected, you see one queue per user and some nifty usage statistics. Notice how the **ack** column is empty. This should be no surprise to you if you remember what we've said about message acknowledgement. You're receiving messages while letting RabbitMQ know we won't be acknowledging them; thus, there's no activity related to acknowledging messages!

Do not fear the multiplication of queues; with enough RAM, a RabbitMQ can deal with hundreds of thousands of queues and bindings without flinching.

Confident about its architecture and implementation, CCM rolls out the user-to-user messaging subsystem to production. It's an immediate success. Users actually want a new feature added to it: the capacity to send a message to a group of users. Let's see how we're going to implement this new feature with RabbitMQ.

Adding topic messages

CCM's application allows users to organize themselves in groups by registering their topics of interest. The new message feature we want to roll out will allow a user to send a message to all users interested in a particular topic. It turns out that this feature matches a specific exchange routing rule, not surprisingly called **topic**! This type of exchange allows the routing of message to all the queues that have been bound with a routing key that matches the routing key of the message. So, unlike the direct exchange that routes a message to at the most one queue, the topic exchange can route it to multiple queues.

> The topic exchange supports strict routing key matching and also wild-card matching using * and # as respective placeholders for exactly one word and zero or more words. Words are delimited by dots, so even if routing keys are of free form, RabbitMQ will interpret dots in them as word separators. It's a good practice to structure routing keys from the most general element to the most specific one, such as news.economy.usa.

The following figure illustrates how the topic exchange will be used in CCM's application. In the following figure, notice how the single inbox queue remains unchanged but simply gets connected to the topic exchange via extra bindings, each of them reflecting the subject of interest of a user:

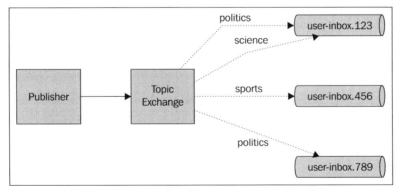

The topic exchange sending thematic messages to users' queues

Because you use the same inbox for everything, the code for fetching messages that is already in place doesn't need to be changed. In fact, this whole feature can be implemented with only a few additions. The first of these additions takes care of declaring the topic exchange in the existing onApplicationStart method as follows:

```
rabbitMqManager.call(new ChannelCallable<DeclareOk>()
{
    @Override
    public String getDescription()
    {
        return "Declaring topic exchange: " +
          USER_TOPICS_EXCHANGE;
    }

    @Override
    public DeclareOk call(final Channel channel)
      throws IOException
    {
        final String exchange = USER_TOPICS_EXCHANGE;
        final String type = "topic";
        // survive a server restart
        final boolean durable = true;
        // keep it even if not in user
        final boolean autoDelete = false;
        // no special arguments
        final Map<String, Object> arguments = null;

        return channel.exchangeDeclare(exchange, type, durable,
          autoDelete, arguments);
    }
});
```

Nothing really new or fancy here; the main difference with the direct exchange you previously declared is that this exchange is named user-topics and is of the type topic. Sending a message is even simpler than with the user-to-user feature because there is no attempt to create the addressee's queue; it wouldn't make sense for the sender to iterate through all the users to create and bind their queues. Only users already subscribed to the target topic at the time of sending will get the message, which is exactly the expected functionality. The sendTopicMessage method is listed hereafter:

```
public String sendTopicMessage(final String topic, final String
message)
{
    return rabbitMqManager.call(new ChannelCallable<String>()
```

```
        {
            @Override
            public String getDescription()
            {
                return "Sending message to topic: " + topic;
            }

            @Override
            public String call(final Channel channel) throws IOException
            {
                String messageId = UUID.randomUUID().toString();

                BasicProperties props = new BasicProperties.Builder()
                    .contentType(MESSAGE_CONTENT_TYPE)
                    .contentEncoding(MESSAGE_ENCODING)
                    .messageId(messageId)
                    .deliveryMode(2)
                    .build();

                // publish the message to the topic exchange
                channel.basicPublish(USER_TOPICS_EXCHANGE, topic, props,
    message.getBytes(MESSAGE_ENCODING));

                return messageId;
            }
        });
    }
```

Except the difference that you will now publish to the user-topics exchange, the rest of the code that creates and publishes the message is exactly the same as the user-to-user messaging. Lastly, we need to add the following method to let the application inform the UserMessageManager when a user subscribes or unsubscribes from certain topics:

```
    public void onUserTopicInterestChange(final long userId,
        final Set<String> subscribes,
        final Set<String> unsubscribes)
    {
        final String queue = getUserInboxQueue(userId);

        rabbitMqManager.call(new ChannelCallable<Void>()
        {
            @Override
            public String getDescription()
            {
```

```
                return "Binding user queue: " + queue + " to exchange: " +
      USER_TOPICS_EXCHANGE + " with: "
                    + subscribes + ", unbinding: " + unsubscribes;
          }

          @Override
          public Void call(final Channel channel) throws IOException
          {
            for (String subscribe : subscribes)
            {
              channel.queueBind(queue,
                USER_TOPICS_EXCHANGE, subscribe);
            }

            for (String unsubscribe : unsubscribes)
            {
              channel.queueUnbind(queue,
                USER_TOPICS_EXCHANGE, unsubscribe);
            }

            return null;
          }
        });
    }
```

Why do we give the responsibility of managing the users' subscription state to the application? Why can't onUserTopicInterestChange be self-contained? The reason is that the AMQP specification does not provide any means to introspect the current bindings of a queue. Therefore, it is not possible to iterate them in to remove the ones not needed anymore in order to reflect a change in a user's topics of interest. This is not a terrible concern because the application is required to maintain this state anyway; it just needs to be sure to inform UserMessageManager when a user's interests change.

> The RabbitMQ management console exposes a **REST API** that can be used to perform queue binding introspection, among other many other features not covered by the AMQP specification.

With this new code in place, everything works as expected. No code change is needed to retrieve messages because they arrive in the same inbox queue as the user-to-user messages. Indeed, topical messages are sent and received correctly by users, and all this with a minimal change and no increase in the number of queues. When connected to the management console, click on the **Exchanges** tab; the only visible difference is the new exchange topic **user-topics**.

The user-topics topic exchange is showing on the management console

Summary

In this chapter, you learned about connecting to RabbitMQ and sending and receiving messages. You also discovered the direct and topic exchanges and put them into motion in the context of CCM's user-to-user and group messaging features.

In the next chapter, we're going to up the ante. CCM will increase responsiveness of the messaging system by switching to server-push and then keep rolling out new features on it.

3
Switching to Server-push

In the previous chapter, you learned how to connect to and get messages from RabbitMQ. Though receiving messages synchronously works perfectly, messages can be "pushed" from RabbitMQ directly to an application consumer for greater efficiency, as you'll discover in this chapter. In the process, you'll also learn how message consumers can either manually acknowledge messages or receive the messages without acknowledgements, the former allowing a zero-message loss design. Finally, you'll be acquainted with the **fanout** exchange, which routes messages to all queues bound to it, irrespective of the routing keys.

In this chapter, you will learn about the following topics:

- Consuming messages from queues
- Manually acknowledging messages
- The fanout exchange

Moving beyond polling

Clever Coney Media is enjoying the application inbox feature that was rolled out in the previous chapter. Users enjoy it very much as well. Everything works fine except for the fact that the frontend regularly polling the backend for messages is starting to take its toll in terms of load, meaning it has begun to suffer performance degradation. Granted, the slow polling mechanism that was initially in place between the frontend and the backend was not designed to perform more than a basic ping. A better approach is needed.

CCM decides to re-architect the solution in favor of a **server-push** approach. The idea is to server-push messages to the users' browsers whenever a message is available, instead of regularly polling to fetch a message or, more often than not, nothing. The good news is that there is a technology perfect for this use case: **WebSocket**. Well supported by modern browsers, this protocol has the advantage of being full-duplex, which means that messages will be able to flow in both directions. Therefore, each frontend to backend WebSocket connection will be used both to server-push messages back to users and also for users to send messages to the server. This is illustrated in the following figure:

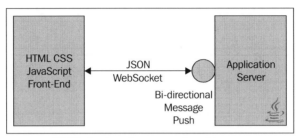

WebSocket-based server-push architecture

It is important to note that both server-push and poller-based mechanisms can coexist pacifically. Indeed, CCM will keep the AJAX endpoint currently used by the poller mechanism in order to support older or less capable browsers. The idea is that if a WebSocket connection can't be established, the frontend will revert to the polling mechanism.

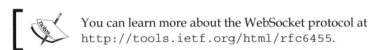

You can learn more about the WebSocket protocol at http://tools.ietf.org/html/rfc6455.

Let's now follow CCM as it rolls out server-push.

Consuming queues

The following diagram illustrates the interactions between the client and server WebSocket peers and the RabbitMQ exchanges and queues:

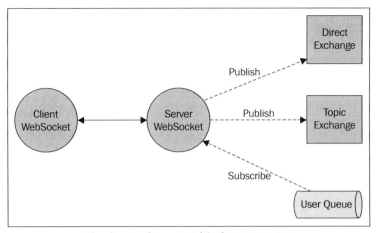

The client and server WebSockets connecting

In the previous diagram, the publication of messages towards the **direct exchange** for user-to-user messages, and the **topic exchange** for group messages, is not different than before. What is different is that instead of getting the messages from RabbitMQ queues, you will **consume** them. What's the difference? When you consume messages, you register a listener that new messages arriving in the queue will be automatically delivered to. So, unlike the synchronous `basicGet` operations you were performing before, you will now be using an asynchronous consumer to receive the queued messages.

Since you're still working on the CCM's application server that is in Java, you will look at RabbitMQ's Java API. Registering a queue consumer is as simple as follows:

```
channel.basicConsume(queue, autoAck, consumer)
```

Here, the consumer is an implementation of the `com.rabbitmq.client.Consumer` interface. The interface defines the contract between a queue consumer and RabbitMQ. It sports several methods, some related to receiving error notifications, but the main method you will focus on is the following:

```
void handleDelivery(String consumerTag,
                    Envelope envelope,
                    AMQP.BasicProperties properties,
                    byte[] body)
    throws IOException;
```

The `handleDelivery` method is called whenever a message is received from the queue. Hence, when this method is called, you will want to push the message back to the frontend via the WebSocket server.

The RabbitMQ Java client comes with a handy default implementation of the `com.rabbitmq.client.Consumer` interface named `com.rabbitmq.client.DefaultConsumer`. Use it and override only the methods you are interested in.

The consumer is bound to the channel that was used to consume a particular queue. If this channel is closed, the consumer will stop receiving messages. Since a channel cannot be reopened and has to be recreated from scratch, the implication is that both the channel and its consumer must be re-established in case of problems. CCM decides to tackle this problem by wrapping the consumer in a class that supports the reconnection mechanism.

Creating a consumer subscription wrapper

CCM decides to create a `Subscription` class to represent a user subscription to its own queue while supporting the possibility of being reconnected. Let's now progressively unfold this class and comment it as we go:

```
public class Subscription
{
    private final static Logger LOGGER = Logger.
getLogger(Subscription.class.getName());

    private final String queue;
    private final SubscriptionDeliverHandler handler;

    private volatile DefaultConsumer consumer;

    public Subscription(final String queue, final
      SubscriptionDeliverHandler handler)
    {
        this.queue = queue;
        this.handler = handler;
    }
```

The state that the `Subscription` class will encapsulate consists of the following:

- queue: This is the queue name that will be consumed to receive user messages
- handler: This is the callback that will be called when a message arrives
- consumer: This is the instance of the consumer, when connected to a channel, declared `volatile` so it can safely be re-created by another thread

At this point, you're probably wondering what the `SubscriptionDeliveryHandler` interface look like. It is as follows:

```
public interface SubscriptionDeliverHandler
{
    void handleDelivery(Channel channel,
                        Envelope envelope,
                        AMQP.BasicProperties properties,
                        byte[] body);
}
```

As you can see, the preceding code exposes only a `handleDelivery` method, which is very similar to the one from RabbitMQ's `Consumer` interface (see http://bit.ly/rmqconsumer), but provides `channel` instead of `consumerTag`. For now, let's just say that CCM doesn't need `consumerTag` but needs the current channel. You'll soon find out why. For now, let's keep on with our discovery of the `Subscription` class. First, let's look at what happens when it's starting:

```
public String start(final Channel channel) throws IOException
{
    consumer = null;

    if (channel != null)
    {
        try
        {
            consumer = new DefaultConsumer(channel)
            {
                @Override
                public void handleDelivery(final String
                  consumerTag,
                    final Envelope envelope,
                    final BasicProperties properties,
                    final byte[] body) throws IOException
                {
                    handler.handleDelivery(channel, envelope,
                      properties, body);
                }
            };

            final boolean autoAck = false;
            final String consumerTag = channel.basicConsume
              (queue, autoAck, consumer);
```

```
            LOGGER.info("Consuming queue: " + queue + ": with tag:
                " + consumerTag + " on channel: "
                            + channel);

            return consumerTag;
        }
        catch (final Exception e)
        {
            LOGGER.log(Level.SEVERE, "Failed to start consuming queue:
    " + queue, e);
            consumer = null;
        }
    }

    return null;
}
```

The notable bits, hidden in Java's typical error-handling drama, are as follows:

- On start, a fresh channel instance is provided
- RabbitMQ's DefaultConsumer keeps a reference to this channel
- Its `handleDelivery` method is directly wired to CCM's own version of `handleDelivery` in the configured handler
- The automatic acknowledgment of messages is turned off (we'll discuss why soon)
- `basicConsume` is the channel method in charge of establishing a consumer instance as the listener of a queue's messages
- The `consumer` field is nullified if the subscription hasn't been activated

Let's delve into the `stop` method right away, as follows:

```
public void stop()
{
    final Channel channel = getChannel();
    if (channel == null)
    {
        return;
    }

    LOGGER.log(Level.INFO, "Stopping subscription: " + this);

    try
    {
        channel.basicCancel(consumer.getConsumerTag());
```

```
    }
    catch (final Exception e)
    {
        LOGGER.log(Level.SEVERE, "Failed to cancel subscription: "
          + this, e);
    }

    try
    {
        channel.close();
    }
    catch (final Exception e)
    {
        LOGGER.log(Level.SEVERE, "Failed to close channel: "
          + channel, e);
    }
    finally
    {
        consumer = null;
    }
}
```

There's not much to it really. With lots of fail-safe mechanisms, this method firstly cancels the active consumer so RabbitMQ stops delivering messages to it, before closing the current channel and nullifying the consumer field. Note that the current channel is extracted from the current consumer via the getChannel method as follows:

```
public Channel getChannel()
{
    return consumer == null ? null : consumer.getChannel();
}
```

You're almost done with this class. Let's take a look at the last two methods:

```
@Override
protected void finalize() throws Throwable
{
    stop();
}

@Override
public String toString()
{
    final ToStringHelper tsh = Objects.toStringHelper(this).
addValue(hashCode()).add("queue", queue);
    if (consumer != null)
```

```
    {
        tsh.add("channel", getChannel());
        tsh.add("consumerTag", consumer.getConsumerTag());
    }
    return tsh.toString();
}
```

The `finalize` method is overridden to ensure that the subscription is closed if for
any reason, the class gets garbage collected before `stop` is properly called. Because
the `stop` method is idempotent, it's fine to call it several times. The `toString` method
is overridden to provide a nice textual rendering of the `Subscription` class.

> Good production-grade systems produce meaningful log entries; strive to
> give enough contexts when you log events in order to simplify forensics
> when something goes wrong, or during development to allow you to
> trace the execution across multiple classes and threads.

The `Subscription` class by itself is not enough to ensure the robustness of the
system because it doesn't contain any reconnection logic. Therefore, its instances
must be "babysat" by an external entity. Let's see how this is done.

Babysitting subscriptions

Being the channel factory of your application, the `RabbitMqManager` class is the
natural factory for `Subscription` instances. Because it creates the subscription
and because it takes care of handling connection issues and reconnections, the
`RabbitMqManager` class is the most appropriate entity for babysitting `Subscription`
instances. The following is how subscriptions are created:

```
private final Set<Subscription> subscriptions;

public RabbitMqManager(final ConnectionFactory factory)
{
    // ... existing code omitted

    subscriptions = synchronizedSet(new HashSet<Subscription>());
}

public Subscription createSubscription(final String queue, final
SubscriptionDeliverHandler handler)
{
    final Subscription subscription = new Subscription
      (queue, handler);
    subscriptions.add(subscription);
```

```
        startSubscription(subscription);
        return subscription;
    }


    private void startSubscription(final Subscription subscription)
    {
        final Channel channel = createChannel();

        if (channel != null)
        {
            try
            {
                subscription.start(channel);
            }
            catch (final Exception e)
            {
                LOGGER.log(Level.SEVERE, "Failed to start
                    subscription: " + subscription + " on channel: "
                                            + channel, e);
            }
        }
    }
```

What is interesting to note is that whether the start operation succeeds or not, a `Subscription` instance will be provided to the caller of `createSubscription`. This opens the door for graceful and transparent reconnections. So how does reconnection actually work? If you remember from the previous chapter, it's the start method of the `RabbitMqManager` that gets called when a reconnection attempt occurs. The only change that was needed to this method was to add a call to `restartSubscriptions`, which is reproduced after the following:

```
private void restartSubscriptions()
{
    LOGGER.info("Restarting " + subscriptions.size() + "
subscriptions");

    for (final Subscription subscription : subscriptions)
    {
        startSubscription(subscription);
    }
}
```

That's it. You can now tie the WebSocket server endpoint with the subscription mechanism.

Tying into the WebSocket endpoint

You first need to refactor the `UserMessageManager` class to expose variants of `sendUserMessage` and `sendTopicMessage` that take a channel argument. Indeed, since you will have an active channel associated with a subscription, you will use it not only to consume messages, but also to produce them.

> Channels are full duplex, which means that one channel can be used for both publishing and consuming messages.

On top of these basic refactorings, you also need to add the following to the UserMessageManager method to allow creating a subscription for a particular user inbox:

```
public Subscription subscribeToUserInbox(final long userId, final
SubscriptionDeliverHandler handler)
{
    final String queue = getUserInboxQueue(userId);
    return rabbitMqManager.createSubscription(queue, handler);
}
```

CCM uses a JSR-356-compliant implementation of server-side WebSocket in its Java application backend. In this model, an application has to expose WebSocket endpoints, so CCM will create one endpoint dedicated to user messaging.

> Here is a good introduction to JSR-356, the Java API for WebSocket:
> `http://www.oracle.com/technetwork/articles/java/`
> `jsr356-1937161.html`.

We will look at the main methods of `UserMessageServerEndpoint`, keeping in mind that WebSocket authentication will not be discussed. Let's first look at what happens when a user browser connects to the WebSocket server:

```
@OnOpen
public void startSubscription(@PathParam("user-id") final long
  userId, final Session session)
{
    session.setMaxIdleTimeout(0);

    final Subscription subscription =
      userMessageManager.subscribeToUserInbox(userId,
        new SubscriptionDeliverHandler()
        {
            @Override
```

```
public void handleDelivery(final Channel channel,
  final Envelope envelope,
  final BasicProperties properties,
  final byte[] body)
{
  try
  {
    final String contentEncoding =
      properties.getContentEncoding();
    session.getBasicRemote().sendText(new String
      (body, contentEncoding));
    channel.basicAck(envelope.getDeliveryTag(),
      false);
  }
  catch (final Exception e)
  {
    LOGGER.log(Level.SEVERE,
      "Failed to push over websocket message ID: " +
        properties.getMessageId(), e);

    try
    {
        final boolean requeue = true;
        channel.basicReject(envelope.getDeliveryTag(),
        requeue);
    }
    catch (final Exception e2)
    {
        LOGGER.log(Level.SEVERE,
          "Failed to reject and requeue message ID:
            " + properties.getMessageId(), e);
    }
  }
});

session.getUserProperties().put
  (RABBITMQ_SUBSCRIPTION, subscription);
}
```

The important aspect of this method is that it uses `userMessageManager` received by the dependency injection, to subscribe `SubscriptionDeliverHandler` that is in charge of sending the messages consumed from the user-specific queue on WebSocket. Do you see how the `channel` instance passed in CCM's custom `handleDelivery` method comes handy? It is required needed to perform manual **message acknowledgement** with the `basicAck` channel action. You perform this single message acknowledgment if and only if the `sendText` WebSocket operation has succeeded (that is, it didn't throw an exception). Otherwise, you use `basicReject` to actively **reject** and **requeue** the delivered message. If you don't acknowledge and fail to reject a message, the RabbitMQ broker will eventually redeliver the message once the subscription is re-established with a new channel.

Use manual acknowledgment if there is a risk that the processing of a message may fail and you want the broker to eventually redeliver it. Redelivery of unacknowledged messages doesn't happen immediately unless the `basicReject` or `basicRecover` channel actions are used. With the automatic acknowledgment mode, it's impossible to reject messages or recover channels.

Also, note how the session's user properties are used to store the subscription so that it can be used in other methods. Indeed, you are required to gracefully terminate the subscription in case of disconnection of the WebSocket, as shown in the following code:

```
@OnClose
public void stopSubscription(final Session session)
{
    final Subscription subscription = (Subscription) session.
getUserProperties().get(
        RABBITMQ_SUBSCRIPTION);

    if (subscription != null)
    {
        subscription.stop();
    }
}
```

Of course, the `Subscription` instance is also required to publish messages because, as you may remember, it acts as a channel provider, as shown in the following code:

```
@OnMessage
public void publishMessage(final String jsonMessage, final Session
    session)
        throws IOException, EncodeException
```

```
{
    final Subscription subscription = (Subscription)
      session.getUserProperties().get(
        RABBITMQ_SUBSCRIPTION);

    final Channel channel = subscription == null ? null :
      subscription.getChannel();
    if (channel == null)
    {
        LOGGER.log(Level.SEVERE, "No active channel to dispatch
          message: " + jsonMessage);
        return;
    }

    // inspect the message to find out where to route it
    final Message message = OBJECT_MAPPER.readValue(jsonMessage,
      Message.class);
    if (message.getAddresseeId() != null)
    {
        userMessageManager.sendUserMessage(message.getAddresseeId(),
          jsonMessage, channel);
    }
    else if (!Strings.isNullOrEmpty(message.getTopic()))
    {
        userMessageManager.sendTopicMessage(message.getTopic(),
          jsonMessage, channel);
    }
    else
    {
        LOGGER.log(Level.SEVERE, "Received unroutable message: " +
          jsonMessage);
    }
}
```

Did you see how you now use the `sendUserMessage` and `sendTopicMessage`
method variants that take a channel as a third argument? There is now no reason
to keep using the somewhat wasteful method of creating and closing the channel
each time since you now have access to a channel, which itself benefits from the
reconnection mechanism you've created.

CCM is now ready to activate server-push for its user messaging feature!

Running the application

CCM has tested whether the server-push mechanism successfully withstands connection issues with the RabbitMQ broker. Its application can start even if it can't connect to the broker, and it can recover if the broker is restarted.

> The robustness of a distributed system isn't the sole responsibility of one actor but a combination of the effort of all its members. No matter how highly available one of its members is, accounting for its potential failure in other members that depend on it will ensure a smooth ride and avoid the proverbial wake-up call.

Let's take a glance at the management console to see how switching to server-push has affected things. The following figure shows the channel's view:

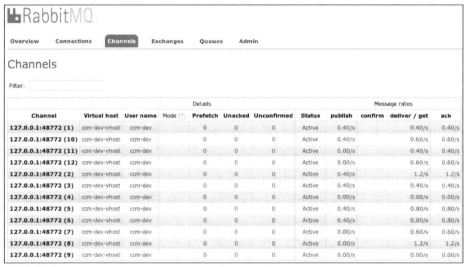

Active consumers keeping channels open

Remember how with the polling approach, where channels were open and closed very quickly, no channel was visible on the view. Now, because each consumer keeps its channel open, you can see active channels in the management console. You can also see the associated usage rates.

> There is no logical limit to the number of channels a RabbitMQ broker can handle; the limiting factors are the available memory on the broker as each channel mobilizes memory, and the actual network bandwidth available for pushing messages on all these channels.

Now, let's take a look at the queue view of the management console:

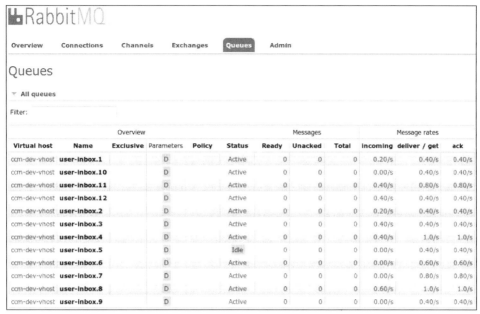

		Overview				Messages			Message rates		
Virtual host	Name	Exclusive	Parameters	Policy	Status	Ready	Unacked	Total	incoming	deliver / get	ack
ccm-dev-vhost	user-inbox.1		D		Active	0	0	0	0.20/s	0.40/s	0.40/s
ccm-dev-vhost	user-inbox.10		D		Active	0	0	0	0.00/s	0.40/s	0.40/s
ccm-dev-vhost	user-inbox.11		D		Active	0	0	0	0.40/s	0.80/s	0.80/s
ccm-dev-vhost	user-inbox.12		D		Active	0	0	0	0.40/s	0.40/s	0.40/s
ccm-dev-vhost	user-inbox.2		D		Active	0	0	0	0.20/s	0.40/s	0.40/s
ccm-dev-vhost	user-inbox.3		D		Active	0	0	0	0.40/s	0.40/s	0.40/s
ccm-dev-vhost	user-inbox.4		D		Active	0	0	0	0.40/s	1.0/s	1.0/s
ccm-dev-vhost	user-inbox.5		D		Idle	0	0	0	0.00/s	0.40/s	0.40/s
ccm-dev-vhost	user-inbox.6		D		Active	0	0	0	0.00/s	0.60/s	0.60/s
ccm-dev-vhost	user-inbox.7		D		Active	0	0	0	0.00/s	0.80/s	0.80/s
ccm-dev-vhost	user-inbox.8		D		Active	0	0	0	0.60/s	1.0/s	1.0/s
ccm-dev-vhost	user-inbox.9		D		Active	0	0	0	0.00/s	0.40/s	0.40/s

Manual acknowledgements showing up in rates

Did you see how the **ack** column shows a non-zero rate? This is because you are now using manual acknowledgment. Thus, the RabbitMQ client now sends `ack` messages over the wire to the broker. This definitely has a cost in terms of bandwidth usage and general performance; however, if in your case, you value the guarantee of successful message processing over speed, it is perfectly acceptable.

After hearing about the resounding success of server-pushed user messages, the customer support team at Clever Coney Media came up with a new requirement: being able to message all users in the system. Let's see how this new feature can be implemented!

Publishing to all queues

CCM's journey with RabbitMQ is just getting more exciting; a new application now wants to integrate with the user's messaging platform! Indeed, the customer support team wants to be able to send messages to all users directly from their back-office application. They are fine with the fact that this public address system will only be able to reach users who have already used the messaging system. This means there's no need to forcefully create queues and bindings for all the existing users of the system; only the really active ones who log in regularly will be reachable.

With this specification in hand, you can start planning and come up with the new overall messaging architecture shown in the following diagram. There's no fundamental change; the only addition is the **Ruby on Rails** back-office application that will be connected to the RabbitMQ in order to publish messages.

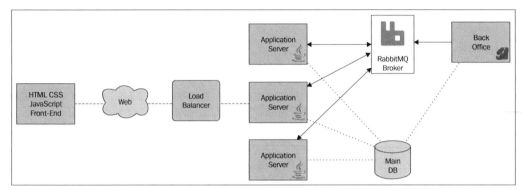

The new architecture with the back-office public address

To roll this out, you can use the topic's messaging that's already in place and create a special `cs-pa` topic to which all users would be subscribed. But in fact, there's a cleaner and simpler approach offered by the AMQP protocol: the fanout exchange. As shown in the following diagram, the fanout exchange routes a copy of each message it receives to all the queues bound to it. This model fits perfectly with the public-address behavior that CCM aims for.

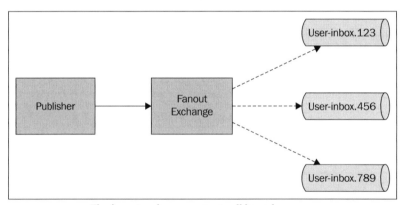

The fanout exchange routes to all bound queues.

With this said, let's wire the fanout exchange in the main Java application.

Binding to the fanout

To start using this new exchange in the main application, you need to perform two steps: declare the fanout exchange when the application starts and bind the user inbox queue to it when a user logs in. So, let's do just that. You will first extend the onApplicationStart method of the UserMessageManager class with the following code:

```
public static final String USER_FANOUT_EXCHANGE = "user-fanout";

rabbitMqManager.call(new ChannelCallable<DeclareOk>()
{
    @Override
    public String getDescription()
    {
        return "Declaring fanout exchange: " +
          USER_FANOUT_EXCHANGE;
    }

    @Override
    public DeclareOk call(final Channel channel)
      throws IOException
    {
        final String exchange = USER_FANOUT_EXCHANGE;
        final String type = "fanout";
        // survive a server restart
        final boolean durable = true;
        // keep it even if not in user
        final boolean autoDelete = false;
        // no special arguments
        final Map<String, Object> arguments = null;

        return channel.exchangeDeclare(exchange, type, durable,
          autoDelete, arguments);
    }
});
```

Once again, you'll use the same set of properties except that this time the exchange type is **fanout**. You then add the following to the onUserLogin method:

```
rabbitMqManager.call(new ChannelCallable<BindOk>()
{
    @Override
    public String getDescription()
    {
```

```
        return "Binding user queue: " + queue + " to exchange: " +
            USER_FANOUT_EXCHANGE;
    }

    @Override
    public BindOk call(final Channel channel) throws IOException
    {
        // bind the addressee's queue to the fanout exchange
        final String routingKey = "";
        return channel.queueBind(queue, USER_FANOUT_EXCHANGE,
            routingKey);
    }
});
```

Did you notice how you used an empty string as the routing key when binding the queue? The value doesn't really matter because the fanout exchange doesn't care about routing keys; however, you can't use `null` so you settled for `""`.

Now you're done; there's nothing more to do as the existing server-push infrastructure will remain the same, especially because users can't publish messages to this fanout exchange. So, let's now turn our attention to the code added to the back office to publish messages on this new exchange.

Publishing to all

CCM's back-office system is a Ruby on Rails application. After looking around, it found several AMQP clients that could be used to connect from Ruby to RabbitMQ. They've selected the one called Ruby AMQP (accessible at `http://rubyamqp.info`) because of its capacity to integrate well with the Rails application and its support for a range of processing models, including Phusion Passenger, which is what they're currently using.

Because this new public address system will be rarely used, you're not concerned about efficient connection management as you are with the main application. In fact, you're fine with connecting and disconnecting for each interaction with the fanout exchange because, if you're having temporary issues with the RabbitMQ broker, retrying to publish from the back-office application will eventually end up working. So, the following is the Ruby code used to publish a message on the public address system:

```
AMQP.connect(:host => '127.0.0.1',
             :username => 'ccm-dev',
             :password => 'coney123',
             :vhost => 'ccm-dev-vhost') do |connection|

    channel  = AMQP::Channel.new(connection)
```

```ruby
exchange = channel.fanout(
    'user-fanout',
    :durable => true,
    :auto_delete => false)

message_id = SecureRandom.uuid
message_json = JSON.generate({
    :time_sent => (Time.now.to_f*1000).to_i,
    :sender_id => -1, # special value for support
    :subject   => pa_subject,
    :content   => pa_content })

exchange.publish(
    message_json,
    :routing_key      => '',
    :content_type     => 'application/vnd.ccm.pmsg.v1+json',
    :content_encoding => 'UTF-8',
    :message_id       => message_id,
    :persistent       => true,
    :nowait           => false) do

    connection.close
end

end
```

The logic in this code should feel familiar; connect to RabbitMQ, get a channel, perform a few channel actions, and then close the connection. You don't need to close the channel before closing the connection; closing the latter closes the former and all other active channels that could have been created on this connection.

Notice that you declare the `user-fanout` exchange right before using it. You do not want to rely on the implicit pre-existence of the exchange as this would necessarily mean the main application would have to run once to create the exchange before the back office can use it. Since exchange declaration is idempotent, you should therefore declare it at all times.

Unless there is a strong guarantee that an exchange or a queue will pre-exist, assume it doesn't exist and declare it. Creating a `happens before` time coupling between two different applications is a recipe for disaster and will blow up at the worst moment. Better to be safe than sorry, especially when AMQP encourages you and provides the necessary means to do so!

Again, you've paid extra attention to make sure the same configuration parameters were used in the exchange declaration than in the Java application.

 Be particularly careful with AMQP client libraries that may use different default values for exchange and queue parameters; it's better to be explicit and to specify all values.

With this code in place, the back-office application can now send public-address messages to all users! This is again a great success, one that again reinforces CCM in its decision to deploy RabbitMQ and build on it.

Running the application

There's nothing spectacular to notice when running the application; messages from the back office successfully flow to the user inbox queues and the only visible change is the newly created **user-fanout** exchange, visible in the management console shown in the following figure:

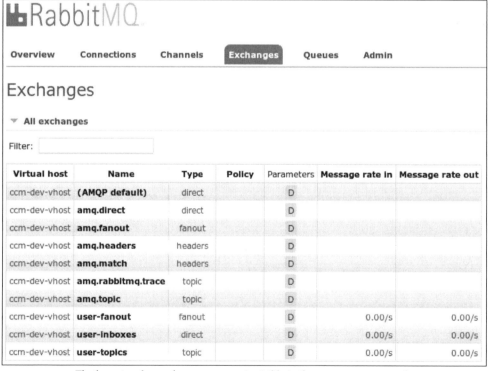

Virtual host	Name	Type	Policy	Parameters	Message rate in	Message rate out
ccm-dev-vhost	(AMQP default)	direct		D		
ccm-dev-vhost	amq.direct	direct		D		
ccm-dev-vhost	amq.fanout	fanout		D		
ccm-dev-vhost	amq.headers	headers		D		
ccm-dev-vhost	amq.match	headers		D		
ccm-dev-vhost	amq.rabbitmq.trace	topic		D		
ccm-dev-vhost	amq.topic	topic		D		
ccm-dev-vhost	user-fanout	fanout		D	0.00/s	0.00/s
ccm-dev-vhost	user-inboxes	direct		D	0.00/s	0.00/s
ccm-dev-vhost	user-topics	topic		D	0.00/s	0.00/s

The fanout exchange for user queues is visible in the management console

At this point, it is very interesting to take a look at the bindings of any particular queue. For this, click on the **Queues** tab and then scroll down and click on **Bindings** to unfold the hidden pane. You should see what's reproduced in the following figure where each queue has multiple bindings, one for the user-to-user messaging feature, several for the topics' messages, and a final one for the public-address fanout feature:

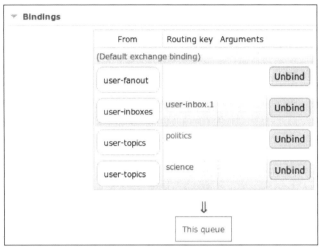

Each user queue has multiple bindings

Before concluding, let's pause for a second and relish the fact that you now have a successful message integration that works across platforms. This may not seem evident to anyone with a little experience with messaging systems, since it is not short of a small miracle. Messaging systems are the realm of platform-specific implementations at best, vendor-locked ones at worst. Thanks to AMQP and RabbitMQ, these Java and Ruby applications can engage in messaging interactions without having to even think about their heterogeneity.

Summary

In this chapter, you learned a new way to consume messages from RabbitMQ. You saw how it can be used to implement snappy server-push messaging in the context of a WebSockets implementation. You also discovered the fanout exchange and how it can be leveraged in order to send a single message to multiple addressees.

But we're not done yet; Clever Coney Media has new plans to use RabbitMQ, plans that will significantly increase the load the broker has to deal with.

Flip to the next chapter to find out what it's up to.

4
Handling Application Logs

RabbitMQ can be used for applications log processing, thanks to its high performance. You're about to learn how to route logs between applications publishing them and custom scripts consuming them. You'll also use the AMQP plugin for JMeter in order to find the performance capacity of consumers. You'll discover that performance can be improved by using message prefetching, a quality of the service property of channels. Finally, you'll see how expressive routing keys can open the door to unexpected new features.

In this chapter, we will discuss the following topics:

- Log concentration with RabbitMQ
- Load testing with JMeter
- Channel quality of service and message prefetching
- Routing key patterns

Publishing and consuming logs

So far, Clever Coney Media has used only RabbitMQ in the context of its main user-facing application. However, others in the company are interested in benefiting from message queuing. If you remember the overview of the architecture that was introduced in *Chapter 1, A Rabbit Springs to Life*, CCM uses Python to perform a data analysis of the user data stored in the different databases being used in the company. The team that is in charge of internal analytics has been looking for an elegant solution to aggregate logs from different applications in order to roll out new statistics, both for internal and end-user consumption.

Taking its interoperable nature into account, CCM thinks that AMQP is the perfect fit for this need; the idea is to publish logs from all applications to RabbitMQ and then use Python to consume, persist, slice, and then dice this data. The following diagram illustrates the architecture it has in mind:

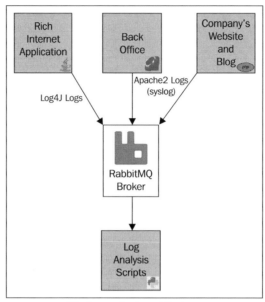

The log analysis architecture

There are two main sources of logs to be dealt with: Log4j for the Java application and syslog for the Apache2-based applications. The team quickly identifies the following two libraries that will facilitate the rolling out of this architecture:

- **Bevis**: This is a syslog listener/server that forwards messages to AMQP (`https://github.com/bkjones/bevis`)

- **AMQP appender**: This is an appender for Log4j that publishes to AMQP (`https://github.com/jbrisbin/vcloud/tree/master/amqp-appender`)

Both these libraries publish logs to topic exchanges and use a configurable routing key that is composed of the level and the source of the log. Let's get to know these routing keys:

- For syslog logs, let the routing key be **severity.facility**, where `severity` is a number between 0 and 7 (the lowest, the most critical) and `facility` is a number between 0 and 23 (`http://tools.ietf.org/html/rfc5424`). Bevis translates these numbers to human-readable values in the routing key. For example, `3.18` gets translated to `err.local2`.

- For Log4j, the routing key is `level.name`, where `level` is a string such as `INFO` or `ERROR`, and `name` is either a fully qualified classname for application-level logs (for instance, `com.ccm.MyClass`), or `access` for access logs.

With such rich routing keys, there is no strong rationale to use a different exchange for each of these two log sources. We will, therefore, configure the libraries to publish to a single topic exchange. It's time to take a look at the implementation!

Pay attention to the expressiveness of the routing keys used with topic exchanges.

Let's start working on the Python script that processes log messages. This script will be in charge of archiving the logs in HDF5, a file format that is well suited for efficiently storing, retrieving, and analyzing swarms of data.

Discussing HDF5 is beyond the scope of this book. You can get more information at `http://www.hdfgroup.org/HDF5/whatishdf5.html`.

The logs' archive script will consume messages from a single queue that will bind to the topic exchange with an all matching routing key (#), as shown in the following diagram:

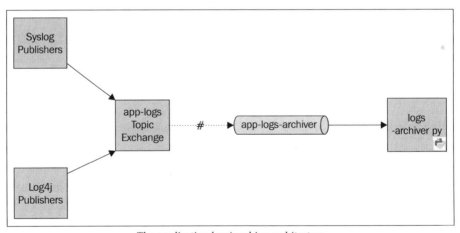

The application logs' archive architecture

If you remember our previous discussion about the notion of *happens before* in the context of declaring exchanges and queues, you should be wondering what program (or programs) will be in charge of these declarations in our current case.

After investigating the syslog and Log4j publishers, it turns out that the former doesn't do any kind of declaration, while the latter declares the exchange in the durable (not-autodelete) mode, but doesn't declare or bind any queue. Consequently, the Python script will have to use the same exchange declaration (which is fine with us as these settings are what we wanted) and will have to create and bind the `app-logs-archiver` queue. To ensure no message gets lost, you will start your Python script before rolling out the syslog and Log4j publishers.

 Always consider publishers' and consumers' exchange and queue declarations and the potential start order they entail.

Let's look at the `logs-archiver.py` script, for which we use the `amqp` library (online documentation available at `http://amqp.readthedocs.org`). Note that in the following code, the `store_log_data` function has been elided for brevity:

```python
#!/usr/bin/env python
import amqp

connection = amqp.Connection(host='ccm-dev-rabbit', userid='ccm-dev',
password='coney123', virtual_host='ccm-dev-vhost')
channel = connection.channel()

EXCHANGE = 'app-logs'
QUEUE = 'app-logs-archiver'

channel.exchange_declare(exchange=EXCHANGE, type='topic',
durable=True, auto_delete=False)
channel.queue_declare(queue=QUEUE, durable=True, auto_delete=False)
channel.queue_bind(queue=QUEUE, exchange=EXCHANGE, routing_key='#')

def handle_message(message):
    store_log_data(message)
    message.channel.basic_ack(delivery_tag=message.delivery_tag)

channel.basic_consume(callback=handle_message, queue=QUEUE, no_
ack=False)

print ' [*] Waiting for messages. To exit press CTRL+C'
while channel.callbacks:
    channel.wait()

channel.close()
connection.close()
```

Thanks to the AMQP specification, this code should look familiar. Indeed, the same concepts are (thankfully) named identically across all the client libraries out there. As you can see, we perform the following tasks:

- Establishing a connection and opening a channel
- Declaring the exchange and queue and binding the latter to the former
- Consuming the queue with a custom callback handler
- Acknowledging messages only when they have been successfully processed (stored, in our case)

The latter point is important; we don't want to risk losing any log message, so the `store_log_data` function should throw an exception. The log message that cannot be handled will be eventually represented for processing. If the error condition is temporary, it will clear up upon redelivery. Otherwise, we will need to address the issue in the code.

Distinguish recoverable from nonrecoverable errors when processing messages in order to redeliver or discard them respectively.

The question you're probably burning to have answered now is: how will this code behave under load? After all, you're about to concentrate all access and application logs of CCM on it! Let's find out with a round of load testing.

Load testing AMQP

You're going to use Apache JMeter with the AMQP plugin to generate load on RabbitMQ. For this first test, your goal is to basically saturate the `logs-archiver.py` script in order to determine what the maximum processing capacity of a single running instance of it. After starting JMeter, add a **Thread Group** element under the **Test Plan** element and configure it as shown in the following screenshot:

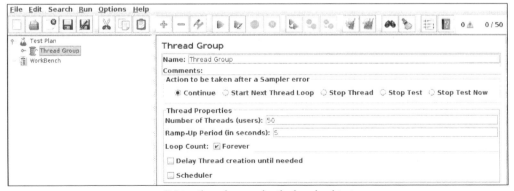

JMeter thread group for the logs load test

As you can see, we will use 50 concurrent threads, each publishing messages to RabbitMQ in an infinite loop. This is way more than the total number of servers at CCM but remember, we want to find out the upper limit of what we can actually achieve. The following screenshot shows the configuration of the element in charge of publishing messages to RabbitMQ by adding an AMQP publisher sampler:

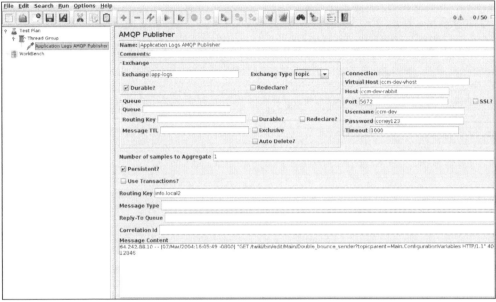

The JMeter AMQP Publisher sampler for the logs load test

Notice how you're simulating an Apache2 syslog message; the routing key is `info.local2` (as per the previous discussion) and the message content is a genuine access log entry. Since none of the log publisher libraries you're using have the message type field, we leave this field blank, which is saddening as we'd rather have all messages sent to RabbitMQ properly stamped with a meaningful type. Also, note that we do not bind any queue on the `app-logs` topic exchange. The responsibility of the load test stops at publishing messages to the right exchange and nothing more.

Keep your load test real; use realistic payload sizes and don't run it all on the localhost. There is a network cost for moving bytes around that you want to have accounted for in your load tests.

The last bit we add is a **Summary Report** listener so that we can follow what's going on when we generate load on RabbitMQ. It doesn't need any configuration and can simply be dropped after the AMQP publisher as shown in the following screenshot:

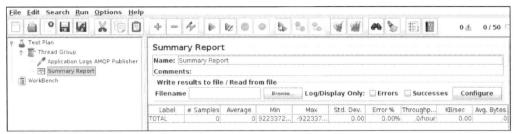

The JMeter Summary Report for the logs load test

That is all! You're ready to load test the log archiver.

Running a load test

After starting the Python script, we start the JMeter load test while having the **Summary Report** open, so we can confirm messages are successfully being sent, as shown in the following screenshot (and yes, the bytes-related statistics, **KB/sec** and **Avg. Bytes**, are buggy):

Label	# Samples	Average	Min	Max	Std. Dev.	Error %	Throughput	KB/sec	Avg. Bytes
Application...	50000	0	0	6	0.17	0.00%	9184.4/sec	17.94	2.0
TOTAL	50000	0	0	6	0.17	0.00%	9184.4/sec	17.94	2.0

The JMeter summary report with the logs load test running

While the test is still running, we connect to the RabbitMQ management console and first look at the **Exchanges** tab. As you can see in the next screenshot, the `app-logs` topic exchange is getting hit pretty hard with more than 7,000 messages per second!

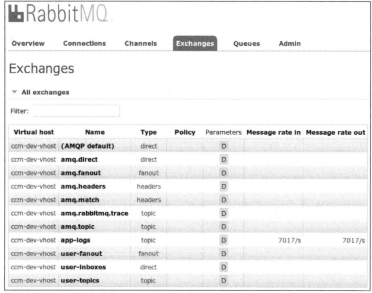

The logs load test generates traffic on the fanout exchange

For us, the most interesting statistics can be seen in the **Queues** tab in the following screenshot:

The logs load test generates traffic on the archiver's queue

Indeed, the Python script is able to receive and acknowledge 766 messages per second. This is 20 times more than what the current CCM infrastructure generates at peak time, which is great. As this means there is enough capacity for CCM's business, the traffic grows significantly. What would we do if one day, this capacity becomes an issue? Remember that you're only running one instance of the archive script; we have the capacity to run several scripts in parallel or refactor it to be multithreaded in order to consume messages from the same queue at a higher rate.

This is great news and a testimony to RabbitMQ's high performance, but you're not over yet. There is another scenario we want to load test — a post-crash recovery.

Prefetching messages

There's a question that lingers at the back of the analyst team's minds: what would happen if the log archiver was off for a while? How long would it take to catch up with the accumulated messages and how can we optimize this recovery time? This is a very important consideration. To answer these questions, we first baseline the existing archive script by sending a fixed number of messages to its queue while it's off then timing how long it takes to catch up.

For this, we modify the JMeter **Thread Group** in order to publish only 50,000 messages, as shown in the following screenshot:

The JMeter Thread Group configured to send 50,000 messages

With this in place, we measure 5,900 milliseconds to consume 50,000 messages with the log archive Python script. This is quite impressive, but is it possible to improve this figure? The answer is yes — thanks to a channel property named **prefetching**, which is part of the **Quality of Service (QoS)** configuration of a channel. This property allows you to configure the number of messages or the amount of bytes (or both) delivered at a time by RabbitMQ to a consumer. Since we acknowledge each message individually, it makes sense that by receiving messages in batches, we will reduce the number of network interactions, thus improving the overall performance.

> The prefetch count and size QoS settings are only effective with manual message acknowledgment.

After several experiments, we find that prefetching messages in batches of 50 provides the maximum improvement. Adding the following line in the logs' archive script effectively lowers the time to 4,083 milliseconds:

```
channel.basic_qos(prefetch_count=50, prefetch_size=0, a_global=False)
```

Note that we do not impose any limit to the number of bytes that can be prefetched by setting the `prefetch_size` to `0`. Also, we do not apply this QoS setting to all channels, only the one used by the log messages' consumer.

> With long-running workers consuming messages from a single queue, set the prefetch count to `1` in order to guarantee a fair distribution of work across your workers.

At this point, you've achieved your targets in terms of capacity estimation and performance improvement. But you're not fully done; while working on the logs' archive script, the team thought of a cool new feature to roll out.

Messaging serendipity

One of the advantages of messaging is that the new behavior that wasn't initially envisioned can easily be grafted to a system because of its lowly coupled nature. In our case, the fact that all application logs are not being published to a single topic exchange allows us to create a specific consumer that will receive only error messages and report them to the operations team.

If you remember our discussion about the routing keys used by the application logs' publishers, all we need to do is to receive messages whose routing first component (that is, the string before the first period of the routing key) indicates an error. These components are as follows:

- For the syslog publisher: `err`, `crit`, `alert`, and `emerg`
- for the Log4j publisher: `ERROR` and `FATAL`

Now we know this, we can create a Python script that will create and bind a queue to the `app-logs` topic exchange, using the one-binding-per-error-message-routing-key pattern. The following code shows the `logs-error-reporter.py` script without the body of the `report_error` function (eluded for brevity):

```python
#!/usr/bin/env python
import amqp

connection = amqp.Connection(host='ccm-dev-rabbit', userid='ccm-dev',
password='coney123', virtual_host='ccm-dev-vhost')
channel = connection.channel()

EXCHANGE = 'app-logs'
QUEUE = 'app-logs-error-reporter'

channel.exchange_declare(exchange=EXCHANGE, type='topic',
durable=True, auto_delete=False)
channel.queue_declare(queue=QUEUE, durable=True, auto_delete=False)

# bind syslog severities:
channel.queue_bind(queue=QUEUE, exchange=EXCHANGE, routing_
key='err.#')
channel.queue_bind(queue=QUEUE, exchange=EXCHANGE, routing_
key='crit.#')
channel.queue_bind(queue=QUEUE, exchange=EXCHANGE, routing_
key='alert.#')
channel.queue_bind(queue=QUEUE, exchange=EXCHANGE, routing_
key='emerg.#')

# bind log4j levels
channel.queue_bind(queue=QUEUE, exchange=EXCHANGE, routing_
key='ERROR.#')
channel.queue_bind(queue=QUEUE, exchange=EXCHANGE, routing_
key='FATAL.#')

channel.basic_qos(prefetch_count=50, prefetch_size=0, a_global=False)

def handle_message(message):
    report_error(message)
    message.channel.basic_ack(delivery_tag=message.delivery_tag)

channel.basic_consume(callback=handle_message, queue=QUEUE, no_
ack=False)

print ' [*] Waiting for messages. To exit press CTRL+C'
while channel.callbacks:
    channel.wait()

channel.close()
connection.close()
```

Notice how you've leveraged the # wildcard in the queue-binding operations that are highlighted in the preceding script. This allows you to match only the first part of the routing key (the severity) and accept anything else after it.

With this script running, let's browse to the **Exchanges** tab of the RabbitMQ management console once more and click on the **apps-log** exchange. The bindings shown in the following screenshot should be visible:

The application logs exchange's multiple bindings

Since you're in the management console, let's do something we haven't done yet. Let's use it to send test messages to the apps-log exchange. Scroll down a little below the **Bindings** section shown in the preceding screenshot until you reach the **Publish message** section. In this interface, fill in the routing key and payload as shown in the following screenshot:

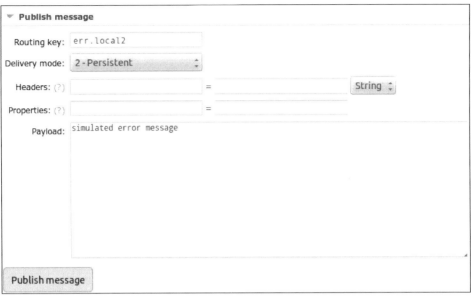

Using the management console to send test log messages

After clicking on **Publish message**, the error gets correctly reported by the Python script. We further test by changing the routing key to info.local2 or ERROR.com.ccm.Tests to see what is reported and what isn't. Everything works as expected, so you're very glad for this last minute idea and the capacity to roll it out cleanly message queuing thanks to RabbitMQ.

Summary

In this chapter, you learned how load testing can be used to determine the maximum capacity of message consumers. You learned about message prefetching and how it can improve the performance for consumers that need to deal with large number of messages. We also explained how messaging can facilitate the rolling out of new and unexpected features in a lowly decoupled architecture.

It seems the team in charge of user messages needs some help to deal with old messages piling up in queues; this is what we'll discuss in the next chapter.

5
Tweaking Message Delivery

While reading the previous chapters, you may have wondered about the fate of messages that are stuck in queues forever. You may even have decided to test the usage of the basic message property named expiration. It's now time to actually tackle the notion of message time-to-live thoroughly. You may also have been wondering whether there was an option to prevent messages that target inexistent queues from being silently dropped. That's also an important question we'll discuss in this chapter.

In this chapter, we will discuss the following topics:

- Message time-to-live
- Dead-letter exchanges and queues
- Mandatory delivery
- Returned message handling

Handling dead letters

Things are going very well at Clever Coney Media. The user messaging feature gets traction as more and more users learn how to use it. After a few months of activity, one thing becomes clear though: some users don't log in to the application often, which leads to messages piling up in their inbox queues. Though the amount of data is not detrimental (yet), the idea of having messages lying around in queues, potentially forever, is not satisfactory. Imagine users logging in after a couple of weeks of vacation and being flooded with obsolete messages—this is the negative type of user experience that CCM is keen on avoiding.

CCM decides to address this by specifying a new rule: after one week, any user message not delivered will be either:

- E-mailed to the user if it's a direct user-to-user message and if the user has opted for an e-mail fallback

- Discarded if it's a topic or a public address message

So, users turn to RabbitMQ to find out what is offered in terms of message expiration. It appears that the following options are possible:

- Using the standard AMQP message `expiration` property for published messages

- Using a custom RabbitMQ extension that allows users to define a message time-to-live (TTL) per queue

- Using a custom RabbitMQ extension that allows users to define a TTL for the queue itself

The first option is interesting because it is a standard AMQP option; however, after reading more about how it is supported in RabbitMQ, it turns out that those messages are only discarded when consumed. Even if expired, they would still sit in the queue, which would defeat the purpose of what they're trying to achieve. CCM rules out the last option because we do not want the queue to be deleted. This leaves the second option: you will configure each user inbox queue with a TTL, which will be enforced by RabbitMQ whether the queue is being consumed or not.

This is all fine and dandy, but what actually happens to messages when they expire? Remember that you want to consume these messages in order to e-mail them. So, how can you achieve this? This is where RabbitMQ's **Dead Letter Exchange (DLX)** comes handy. In messaging parlance, a dead letter is a message that can't be delivered, either because its intended target fails to be achieved or because it expires (typically, a message property indicates the exact failure reason). Thus, in your case, messages that reach their TTL will become dead letters. RabbitMQ offers the option to automatically route these dead letters to a specific exchange, a so-called dead letter exchange. Since you want to receive messages sent to this exchange, you will have to bind a queue to it, consume it, and log received messages. This queue will act as what's known as a **Dead Letter Queue (DLQ)**, the ultimate destination of dead letters. The following diagram illustrates the overall architecture that CCM intends to roll out.

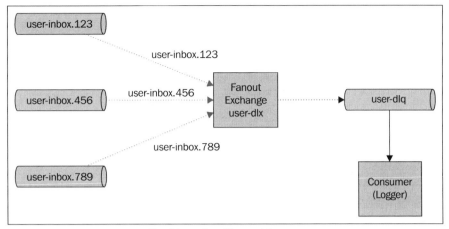

Dead letter handling architecture

What's notable in this diagram is that when they expire, messages published to the DLX use the original routing key they had when they were delivered to a user inbox queue. This behavior can be modified as RabbitMQ allows the definition of a specific routing key to use when messages are published to the DLX. You're happy with the default behavior; the original routing key is an interesting bit of information you'd like to use in order to find out the ID of the concerned user. Therefore, you've made the DLX exchange a fanout one in order to have all messages routed in the DLQ, whatever their original routing key could have been.

The battle plan is ready. It's now time to roll it out!

Refactoring queues

The first step to roll out this architecture consists of configuring the user inbox queues with the desired TTL of one week and a DLX equal to "user-dlx". Using the RabbitMQ extensions to AMQP, this can be achieved by respectively defining the `"x-message-ttl"` and `"x-dead-letter-exchange"` arguments when declaring the queue.

You could be tempted to jump right to your code editor and modify the `declareUserMessageQueue` method to use the following arguments:

```
arguments.put("x-message-ttl", TimeUnit.DAYS.toMillis(7L));
arguments.put("x-dead-letter-exchange", USER_DL_EXCHANGE);
```

However, this would be wrong at several levels. The main issue is that you would be changing the declaration from a queue with no arguments to one with two arguments. Remember our discussion in *Chapter 2, Creating an Application Inbox*, queue (or exchange) declaration is idempotent only if all the parameters used are the same. Any discrepancy in the declaration will yield an exception and will be punished with an immediate channel termination!

Cultivating a "Spidey sense" for breaking changes in queues and exchange declarations will save you the unpleasant experience of repeated errors and the mass extinction of channels.

The other problem is that this change will only apply when users log in. Indeed, this is when we declare the user inbox queue. This would not fulfill our requirement to apply our expiration rule to all existing queues independent of user actions. Finally, another thing to consider is that if these properties were configured at the queue declaration level, any change to one of them will require deleting and recreating all the queues. Clearly, the TTL and DLX configurations are cross-cutting concerns and should rather be configured in a more global fashion. Is that even possible?

The answer is yes! RabbitMQ has a simple and elegant solution to this problem called **policies**. RabbitMQ supports policies that define specific behaviors and that can be applied to queues or exchanges. Policies are applied not only when a queue or exchange is declared, but also to an existing queue or exchange. Both queue message TTL and dead letter exchange are configurable via policies, but only a single policy can apply to a queue or exchange. So, you will craft a policy that combines both TTL and DLX settings and apply it to all user inbox queues. This cannot be achieved via the AMQP protocol, so you can't do this using the RabbitMQ client. You'll instead use the powerful command-line tools provided with RabbitMQ (should you want to do it by code, the management REST API would be your friend). This strategy to refactor the existing queues is achieved with the following single command-line operation:

```
$ sudo rabbitmqctl set_policy -p ccm-dev-vhost Q_TTL_DLX "user-
  inbox\.\d+" '{"message-ttl":604800000, "dead-letter-
  exchange":"user-dlx"}' --apply-to queues
```

Let's take some time to dissect the preceding command:

- `sudo rabbitmqctl set_policy`: This part of the command uses the `set_policy` control command

- `-p ccm-dev-vhost`: This part of the command applies the message to the development virtual host

- `Q_TTL_DLX`: This part of the command names the message so that we understand it pertains to queue time-to-live and dead letter exchange

- `"user-inbox\.\d+"`: This part of the command uses some regex fu to apply the entire command to the user inbox queues only by selecting them by name

- `'{"message-ttl":604800000, "dead-letter-exchange":"user-dlx"}'`: This part of the command uses a policy definition composed of a TTL of seven days in milliseconds and the name of the DLX

- `--apply-to queues`: This part of the command ensures that this policy is only applied to queues, which is somewhat redundant with the regex, but acts as a safety net because it selects RabbitMQ entities by type instead of name

So here we go! You can run this command and life will be peachy. Wait a second! At this time, you haven't created the `"user-dlx"` exchange and you haven't bound the `"user-dlq"` queue to it yet. If you apply this policy right now, you will have seven days to roll out the missing exchange and queue. Sure, this is plenty of time, but smart developers don't like to work against the clock if they can avoid it.

Since you're smart, you're not going to run this command right now. Instead, you'll first create the infrastructure in charge of dealing with the dead letters and roll it out to our application. Then and only then will you apply the `"Q_TTL_DLX"` policy.

Undertaking messages

You need to create the necessary infrastructure to deal with expired messages, which means you need to do the following:

1. Declare the `user-dlx` fanout exchange.

2. Declare the `user-dlq` queue and bind it to the `user-dlx` fanout.

3. Create a subscriber of the `user-dlq` queue that consumes and e-mails the dead letters.

To implement this behavior, you will add extra code to the `onApplicationStart` method of the `UserMessageManager` class. First, you'll add the following code to create the exchange and bind the queue to it:

```
static final String USER_DL_EXCHANGE = "user-dlx";
static final String USER_DL_QUEUE = "user-dlq";

rabbitMqManager.call(new ChannelCallable<BindOk>()
{
    @Override
    public String getDescription()
    {
```

```
        return "Declaring dead-letter exchange: " +
            USER_DL_EXCHANGE + " and queue: " + USER_DL_QUEUE;
    }

    @Override
    public BindOk call(final Channel channel) throws IOException
    {
        final boolean durable = true;
        final boolean autoDelete = false;

        final String exchange = USER_DL_EXCHANGE;
        final String type = "fanout";
        final Map<String, Object> arguments = null;

        channel.exchangeDeclare(exchange, type, durable,
            autoDelete, arguments);

        final String queue = USER_DL_QUEUE;
        final boolean exclusive = false;
        channel.queueDeclare(queue, durable, exclusive,
            autoDelete, arguments);

        final String routingKey = "";
        return channel.queueBind(queue, exchange, routingKey);
    }
});
```

As you can see, this is just a standard fanout exchange declaration and the related queue declaration and binding. You used the same logic while implementing the public address system in *Chapter 3, Switching to Server-push*. Now let's look at the following consumer code for this queue, the code that you're also adding to the onApplicationStart method:

```
rabbitMqManager.createSubscription(USER_DL_QUEUE, new
SubscriptionDeliveryHandler()
{
    @Override
    public void handleDelivery(final Channel channel,
                               final Envelope envelope,
                               final BasicProperties properties,
                               final byte[] body)
    {
        @SuppressWarnings("unchecked")
```

```java
        final List<Map<String, LongString>> deathInfo =
            (List<Map<String, LongString>>)
            properties.getHeaders().get("x-death");

    if(deathInfo.get(0).get("exchange").toString().equals("user-
        inboxes"))
        {
            final long userId =
                Long.valueOf(StringUtils.substringAfter
                (envelope.getRoutingKey(), "user-inbox."));

            final String contentEncoding =
                properties.getContentEncoding();

            try
            {
                final String jsonMessage = new String(body,
                    contentEncoding);
                userManager.handleDeadMessage(userId,
                    jsonMessage);
            }
            catch (final UnsupportedEncodingException uee)
            {
                LOGGER.severe("Failed to handle dead message: " +
                    envelope.getRoutingKey() + ", encoding: " +
                    contentEncoding + ", entry: " +
                    Base64.encodeBase64(body));
            }
        }

        try
        {
            final boolean multiple = false;
            channel.basicAck(envelope.getDeliveryTag(), multiple);
        }
        catch (final IOException ioe)
        {
            LOGGER.severe("Failed to acknowledge: " +
                ToStringBuilder.reflectionToString(envelope,
                ToStringStyle.SHORT_PREFIX_STYLE));
        }
    }
});
```

There's a lot happening here, so let's take some time to focus on the important aspects. The overall structure of the method should look familiar. Indeed, you're reusing the same subscription management feature you've created to consume user messages in the WebSocket (refer to *Chapter 3, Switching to Server-push*). Hurray to code reusage!

You may be puzzled by the very first line of code in the `handle` method. We create a `deathInfo` variable by fetching a message header named `x-death`. Do you remember we said messages sent to the DLX can retain their original routing key? Well, there's something else that happens to them: RabbitMQ injects a custom header name `x-death`, which contains extra contextual information about the cause of death. This extra header is a key-value map with the following entries:

* `queue`: This indicates the queue name where the message was stored before it expired

* `exchange`: This indicates the exchange that this message was sent to

* `reason`: This indicates whether the message is rejected, the TTL for the message has expired, or the queue length limit is exceeded

* `time`: This indicates the date and time when the message was dead lettered

* `routing keys`: This indicates all the routing keys associated with the message (RabbitMQ supports multiple routing keys in an extension to AMQP known as the sender-selected destination, which is beyond the scope of this book and is fully documented at `http://www.rabbitmq.com/sender-selected.html`)

With this map in hand, you can get the original exchange and compare it to see if it's the `user-inboxes` one. In this way, you will only trigger user-specific logic to deal with dead messages for user-to-user messages. All other messages are just directly acknowledged after being consumed, effectively draining the DLX until it's empty. The user ID is extracted from the routing key in order to call the `userManager.handleDeadMessage` method in charge of e-mailing the message to the user if he or she has opted for it.

Note that the reason of death could be used to further filter messages. Here you've assumed only `expired` ones will hit the DLQ; however, in the future, you may roll out new policies that could make messages die for other reasons, such as the incapacity to be delivered.

> Extracting the user ID from the routing key is borderline hackish. A cleaner approach would consist of adding the target user ID in a custom header for user-to-user messages.

Finally, pay attention to how the message bytes get logged when they can't properly be decoded to a string. They're encoded in base 64, which is always possible, and logged alongside the encoding, providing you with enough information to understand the issue.

 Make your life easier and log enough contextual data when an exception occurs. Always consider what information you'll need if you need to perform forensics for a particular exception.

After rolling out this code to your application servers, you will see that the dead letter exchange and queue have been correctly created. Now you can set the "Q_TTL_DLX" policy, as shown in the following code:

```
$ sudo rabbitmqctl set_policy -p ccm-dev-vhost Q_TTL_DLX "user-inbox\.\
d+" '{"message-ttl":604800000, "dead-letter-exchange":"user-dlx"}'
--apply-to queues
Setting policy "Q_TTL_DLX" for pattern "user-inbox\\.\\d+" to
"{\"message-ttl\":604800000, \"dead-letter-exchange\":\"user-dlx\"}" with
priority "0" ...
...done.
```

After running this script, you can use the management console to see what's been changed on the user inbox queue definitions. The following screenshot shows a few of these queues:

RabbitMQ

Overview Connections Channels Exchanges **Queues** Admin

Queues

▼ All queues

Filter:

			Overview				Messages			Message rates	
Virtual host	Name	Exclusive	Parameters	Policy	Status	Ready	Unacked	Total	Incoming	deliver / get	ack
ccm-dev-vhost	user-dlq		D		Idle	0	0	0	0.00/s	0.00/s	0.00/s
ccm-dev-vhost	user-inbox.1		D	Q_TTL_DLX	Idle	0	0	0	0.00/s	0.00/s	0.00/s
ccm-dev-vhost	user-inbox.10		D	Q_TTL_DLX	Idle	0	0	0	0.00/s	0.00/s	0.00/s
ccm-dev-vhost	user-inbox.11		D	Q_TTL_DLX	Idle	0	0	0	0.00/s	0.00/s	0.00/s
ccm-dev-vhost	user-inbox.12		D	Q_TTL_DLX	Idle	0	0	0	0.00/s	0.00/s	0.00/s
ccm-dev-vhost	user-inbox.13		D	Q_TTL_DLX	Idle	0	0	0	0.00/s	0.00/s	0.00/s
ccm-dev-vhost	user-inbox.2		D	Q_TTL_DLX	Idle	0	0	0	0.00/s	0.00/s	0.00/s
ccm-dev-vhost	user-inbox.3		D	Q_TTL_DLX	Idle	0	0	0	0.00/s	0.00/s	0.00/s
ccm-dev-vhost	user-inbox.4		D	Q_TTL_DLX	Idle	0	0	0	0.00/s	0.00/s	0.00/s
ccm-dev-vhost	user-inbox.5		D	Q_TTL_DLX	Idle	0	0	0	0.00/s	0.00/s	0.00/s
ccm-dev-vhost	user-inbox.6		D	Q_TTL_DLX	Idle	0	0	0	0.00/s	0.00/s	0.00/s
ccm-dev-vhost	user-inbox.7		D	Q_TTL_DLX	Idle	0	0	0	0.00/s	0.00/s	0.00/s
ccm-dev-vhost	user-inbox.8		D	Q_TTL_DLX	Idle	0	0	0	0.00/s	0.00/s	0.00/s
ccm-dev-vhost	user-inbox.9		D	Q_TTL_DLX	Idle	0	0	0	0.00/s	0.00/s	0.00/s

The Q_TTL_DLX policy is applied to all user inbox queues

As you can see in the following screenshot, it's clearly visible that the **Q_TTL_DLX** policy has been applied to user inbox queues, while other queues such as the user-dlq haven't been affected. In the management interface, let's click on the **Admin** tab and then the **Policies** tab (on the right). Notice how the custom policy is visible in the following screenshot:

The Q_TTL_DLX details are visible in the management console

At this point, any message created and that will stay for more than seven days in a user queue will be unmercifully moved to the DLQ, consumed, potentially e-mailed, and buried for real! But what should be done with the existing messages that were created before you rolled out the policy? There is, unfortunately, no out-of-the-box solution to this problem, so you will have to take a somewhat drastic measure — you will purge all the queues that are not empty and that have no active subscribers. This is rough, but is your only way to get out of the current conundrum. Moreover, it's a solution you can easily implement with a simple script.

So far, we've been using the rabbitmqctl script to manage our RabbitMQ broker. You need to install a new script that comes bundled with the management console you installed in *Chapter 1, A Rabbit Springs to Life*. This script called rabbitmqadmin can be downloaded by simply browsing a particular URL of the management interface, namely http://localhost:15672/cli/. After following the displayed download instructions, install the script in a location that makes it available to all users (typically, /usr/local/bin on a Linux machine).

 More information on the rabbitmqadmin script can be found at http://www.rabbitmq.com/management-cli.html.

You can now create a script that will drop all consumerless queues that are not empty, as shown in the following code:

```
#!/bin/bash

queues_to_purge=`rabbitmqctl list_queues -p ccm-dev-
vhost name messages_ready consumers | grep "user-inbox\.
[[:digit:]]\+[[:space:]]\+[1-9][[:digit:]]*[[:space:]]\+0" | awk '{
print $1}'`

for queue in $queues_to_purge ; do
    echo -n "Purging $queue ... "
    rabbitmqadmin -V ccm-dev-vhost -u ccm-admin -p hare123 purge
        queue name=$queue
done
```

Notice that you used both `rabbitmqctl` and `rabbitmqadmin` to achieve your goal, the former having the capacity to list specific attributes of queues in a way that's easy to parse, the latter having the capacity to purge queues. After executing this script as a super user, the state of the RabbitMQ broker is where you wanted it and your TTL and DLX policy will keep it that way in the long run!

Sending this message to the e-mail bridge gives a new idea to the customer support team.

Making delivery mandatory

So far, the customer support team at CCM has been relying only on e-mails to interact with individual users. They've recently added the RabbitMQ-powered public address system discussed in *Chapter 3, Switching to Server-push*. Now that direct user messages can get routed to users by e-mails, they're interested in the possibility of sending such messages to individual users from the back office application. Furthermore, if possible they would like users who don't have an inbox queue on RabbitMQ to get the message e-mailed to them immediately instead of having to wait for the seven days' TTL.

In terms of messaging architecture, you're in a known territory; this is the exact same model as the one you put in place in *Chapter 2, Creating an Application Inbox*, for user-to-user messages, as illustrated in the following screenshot. The only difference is that, unlike the main application, the back office will not create and bind a user queue prior to sending a message. Instead, the back office will have to somewhat detect that no such queue pre-exists and revert to an e-mail delivery for the message.

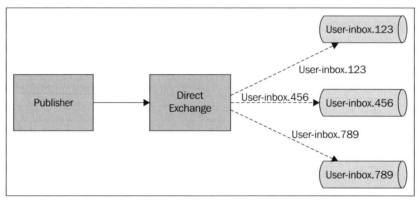

The back office will use the user-inboxes direct exchange for direct messages

What's unclear is how to achieve the second part of the requirements: how can the back office check the pre-existence of a queue? The AMQP specification doesn't define a direct way to do this. The RabbitMQ management plugin exposes a REST API that could be used to check the existence of a queue; it's a tempting approach, but you'd rather stay within the confines of what AMQP offers by default. Moreover, this could expose you to a *check then act* type of race condition. Indeed, the queue could be created by another process after you verify that it doesn't exist. So, after digging deeper into the AMQP specification, you're excited to discover a feature that allows you to achieve your goal in a safe and elegant manner. This feature is called mandatory delivery.

 Consider the management REST API of RabbitMQ for cases when AMQP doesn't have any way to support the functionality you're after. You can access the REST API documentation on your RabbitMQ broker at http://localhost:15672/api/.

When a message is published on an exchange with the *mandatory* flag set to `true`, it will be *returned* by RabbitMQ if the message cannot be delivered to a queue. A message cannot be delivered to a queue either because no queue is bound to the exchange, or because none of the bound queues have a routing key that would match the routing rules of the exchange. In the current case, it would mean that no user inbox queue is bound to a routing key that matches the addressee's user ID.

AMQP defines another delivery-related flag named **immediate**, which is a step beyond **mandatory** in the sense it ensures that the message has been actually delivered to a consumer. RabbitMQ has chosen not to support this feature for it is nontrivial to implement efficiently and elegantly, especially in clustered environments.

The trick about returned messages is that RabbitMQ doesn't return them synchronously as a response to the publish operation; it returns them in an asynchronous fashion. This means that for the developer, a specific message handler will have to be registered with RabbitMQ in order to receive the returned messages. This leads to the overall architecture illustrated in the following diagram:

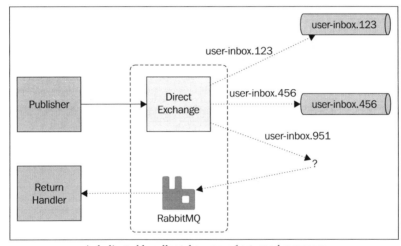

A dedicated handler takes care of returned messages

 If you come from a JMS background, you're probably wondering about transactional delivery. AMQP supports the notion of transactions on a per-channel basis, both for consumers and producers. That said, it comes with several nontrivial "gotchas", due to a certain lack of clarity in the specification. Generally speaking, the acknowledgment/rejection mechanism is preferred for transactions.

With this decided, it's now time to add the necessary code in the back office.

Implementing the back-office sender

In CCM's back office, you're going to add a method very similar to the one used for the public address messaging system (seen in *Chapter 3, Switching to Server-push*); however, this time we will add support for returned messages. The Ruby client library supports this feature very elegantly as you'll soon find out. The following code is the code you need to add to support the mandatory delivery of messages to user inboxes and to handle potentially returned messages. The method that takes care of e-mailing the messages to the users has not been included for brevity, as follows:

```ruby
channel  = AMQP::Channel.new(connection)
exchange = channel.direct(
    'user-inboxes',
    :durable => true,
    :auto_delete => false) do |exchange, declare_ok|
  exchange.on_return do |basic_return, metadata, payload|
    email_message_to_user(payload)
  end
  message_id = SecureRandom.uuid
  message_json = JSON.generate({
    :time_sent => (Time.now.to_f*1000).to_i,
    :sender_id => -1, # special value for support
    :addressee_id => user_id,
    :subject  => 'Direct message from CS',
    :content  => 'A private message from customer support...'})
  routing_key = "user-inbox.#{user_id}"

  exchange.publish(
    message_json,
    :routing_key      => routing_key,
    :content_type     => 'application/vnd.ccm.pmsg.v1+json',
    :content_encoding => 'UTF-8',
    :message_id       => message_id,
    :persistent       => true,
    :nowait           => false,
    :mandatory        => true) do
    puts "Published message ID: #{message_id} to: #{routing_key}"
  end
end
```

In case you don't recall the code used for sending to the public address fanout exchange, we highlighted the lines that differ in this code. In short, the main notable points are as follows:

- The `user-inboxes` direct exchange is used for message publication
- Returned messages are handled through a closure registered via `exchange.on_return`
- The message JSON payload now defines an `addressee_id` field, which is required by the schema for direct user messages
- Messages are published with the required `routing_key` to target a particular user inbox and with the `mandatory` flag set to `true`

That is all! The feature is ready to go live. As you can see, the major "gotcha" was in understanding that messages are returned asynchronously and need to be handled that way.

 The Ruby AMQP library gives the impression that returned messages are provided by exchanges. Behind the scenes, they are actually provided directly by the channels, as it's clearly visible in the RabbitMQ Java client.

Summary

While rolling out two new cool features for Clever Coney Media, you learned about the very important subjects: message TTL and the handling of dead letters with specific exchanges and queues. You discovered the notion policy and how it allows you to refactor your existing queues. You also learned about how delivery can be made mandatory and how to deal with cases when it doesn't succeed.

So far, we've only discussed asynchronous interactions with RabbitMQ, which makes sense because it's the core premise of messaging. That said, it's possible to perform synchronous invocations too, as you're just about to find out in the next chapter.

6
Smart Message Routing

So far, all the messaging interactions that you've learned about were one way: flowing from message publishers to consumers. However, what if the consumer would like to let the publisher know that processing is complete? If the consumer were to act as a service and the publisher as a client, you would have to find a way to route a response back to the consumer. If you've been toying with these questions, then you've arrived at the right chapter! By the end of it, you'll know everything you need to roll out a message-driven, service-oriented architecture. Loose coupling and its related benefits in scalability and graceful degradation will be no mystery to you.

In this chapter, we will discuss the following topics:

- Request-response interaction with reply-to queues
- Exclusive queues
- Advanced routing with headers exchange

Service-oriented messaging

Clever Coney Media has considered rolling out a service-oriented architecture (**SOA**) several times, but never actually did so, mostly out of the fear of introducing tight coupling between their different systems. As their understanding of messaging grew with the use of RabbitMQ, CCM realized that they could benefit from such a message-oriented middleware in their SOA strategy. Their initial assumption was that SOA meant web services that were reductive. Indeed, message queuing can also be used for interacting with services.

To kick-start their RabbitMQ-powered SOA initiative, CCM decided to start with a simple service that would expose the authentication mechanism of the main Java application. This was done to allow other applications to perform login and logout operations with end-user credentials. The first application to benefit from this will be the Ruby on Rails back office. This will allow customer service representatives to test user credentials from within the back office.

A question that should be on your mind by now is: how can we possibly have service-style request-response interactions with RabbitMQ, knowing all the efforts made by AMQP to decouple the publisher from the consumer? You are right to wonder about this. All interactions with RabbitMQ are one way and asynchronous. On the other hand, a client interacting with a service expects to receive a response. How can we resolve this dichotomy? The answer is by reversing the publisher and consumer roles for the response phase. When sending the service request, the client will act as a publisher and the service as a consumer, but when returning the service response, the service will act as a publisher and the client as a consumer. This implies that different queues will be used for requests and responses. This architecture is illustrated in the following diagram:

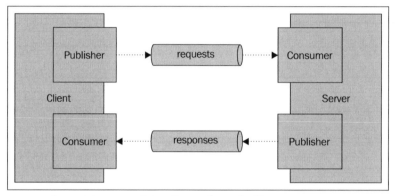

A request-response interaction performed with message queues

 If you have been exposed to document/literal SOAP over JMS, all this should sound very familiar. The only difference is that here we will be using JSON messages and AMQP.

Replying to queues

The other question you probably have right now is: how can the service know where to publish the response message? We can't reasonably hardcode an exchange and routing key in the service to publish responses; it would be too inflexible. The solution is to have the request message carry the coordinates of the location where the response should be sent. The good news is that this mechanism is supported by the AMQP protocol out of the box. If you remember our discussion about the AMQP message structure in *Chapter 2, Creating an Application Inbox*, each message carries a **reply-to** property where the client will store the queue name of the location where the response must be sent.

Wait a minute! Messages are published to exchanges. So, how could you possibly send the response directly to a queue? Well, there's a little trick that we've been hiding from you until now. Every time you create a queue, it gets automatically bound to the default exchange with its queue name as the routing key. This means that by publishing a message to the default exchange using the queue name as the routing key, the message will end up in the designated queue. What is this mysterious default exchange? It's a direct and durable exchange named " " (an empty string) that is automatically created by RabbitMQ for each virtual host. To make the default exchange visible in the management console, its empty string name is rendered as **(AMQP default)**, as shown in the following screenshot:

Virtual host	Name	Type	Policy	Parameters	Message rate in	Message rate out
ccm-dev-vhost	**(AMQP default)**	direct		D		
ccm-dev-vhost	**amq.direct**	direct		D		
ccm-dev-vhost	**amq.fanout**	fanout		D		
ccm-dev-vhost	**amq.headers**	headers		D		
ccm-dev-vhost	**amq.match**	headers		D		
ccm-dev-vhost	**amq.rabbitmq.trace**	topic		D		
ccm-dev-vhost	**amq.topic**	topic		D		

The default exchange is one among several built-in exchanges

As you can see in the preceding screenshot, there are a bunch of other predeclared exchanges that get automatically created for every virtual host. You can spot them easily because their names start with amq.. They are meant for testing and prototyping purposes only, so you do not need to use them in your actual application code.

 With great power comes great responsibility; producing messages to the default exchange is a convenient way to send messages directly to a particular queue. However, don't overuse this pattern! It creates tight coupling between producers and consumers because the producer becomes aware of particular queue names. This basically voids the benefits of having the layer of indirection, thus generating isolation, which is provided by exchanges and their routing rules. Use with care!

You may be wondering what type of queue can be used for the reply-to mechanism? The answer is: any type, but in practice, the following two approaches are used:

- **Create a short-lived queue for each request-response interaction**: This approach uses an exclusive, autodelete, nondurable, and server-side named queue created by the client. It's exclusive so that no other consumer can get messages from it, which makes sense because only the client is supposed to consume the response replied to the queue. It can be autodeleted because once the reply has been consumed, there is no longer a use for it. It doesn't need to be durable because request-response interactions are not meant to be long lived. So, it doesn't matter if unconsumed response messages get lost; the client process waiting for that particular response is long gone. Finally, the responsibility to generate a unique name for this short-lived queue is left to the server, which relieves the client from having to figure out a unique naming scheme.

- **Use a permanent reply-to queue specific to the client**: This approach uses a nonexclusive, nonautodelete, nondurable, and client-side named queue. It is basically a typical queue, except that it doesn't need to be durable for the same reason explained in the previous point. It cannot be exclusive because a different consumer will be used for each request-response interaction. The difficulty in using such a queue is correlating responses with requests. This is done by using the CorrelationId message property that gets carried from the request message to the response message, thus allowing the client to consume the response for the correct request.

The latter approach is more efficient than the former since no queue gets created and then deleted for each request. In your case, since the interactions with the authentication service will be few and far between, you've opted for the first approach. Moreover, the first approach doesn't deal with response correlation, so it's easier to roll out.

 Don't go bare bones if you decide to use permanent reply queues. RabbitMQ client libraries offer primitives that simplify responses that are correlated with requests.

By now, you must have a good idea of how responses will be routed back to response queues, but what about requests? How will we deliver them to the authentication service? Read on as we're about to discover the fourth type of exchange offered by RabbitMQ.

Routing service requests

CCM has two main requirements when it comes to routing request messages
to services:

- Clients should send service requests to a single exchange so that they don't
  have to deal with a map of services to exchanges

- Several versions of the same service should be able to run in parallel to allow
  the graceful evolution of their SOA

With these requirements in mind, your initial thought is probably to use a topic
exchange and structure the routing key as `{service_name}{version}`. This is a
good idea and it would actually work, but RabbitMQ supports a type of exchange
that you haven't used before and that offers a more elegant solution to this problem.
Indeed, the **headers** exchange allows routing messages based on their headers,
which are custom key-value pairs stored in the message properties. This is more
elegant because the routing is guided by the properties of the message and not by
whatever routing key was used at the time of publication. With this approach, the
message and its routing information are all self-contained, remain consistent, and are
therefore easier to inspect as a whole.

The following diagram summarizes the approach we've just discussed in detail:

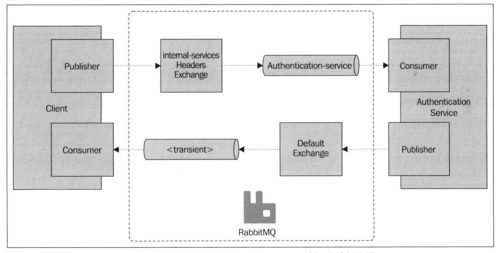

A request-response interaction powered by RabbitMQ

That was a lot of preliminary. By now, you must be eager to see some code. Let's not
further delay it and implement the authentication service first.

Exposing the authentication service

Your first move towards rolling out the authentication service is to create the definition of the request and response messages used for the authentication service. Since CCM favors JSON as a wire format, you're using the JSON schema to strictly define the schemas of the login request and response messages and the logout request and response messages (these schemas can be found in *Appendix, Message Schemas*).

With this done, you can now turn to coding and start by creating a new class unsurprisingly named `AuthenticationService`. It will take care of the communication with RabbitMQ and the dispatch to the internal classes that are actually performing the authentication. Let's look at the first part of the constructor of this class, where we've highlighted the interesting bits:

```
private static final String INTERNAL_SERVICES_EXCHANGE = "internal-
services";
private static final String AUTHENTICATION_SERVICE_QUEUE =
"authentication-service";

public AuthenticationService(final RabbitMqManager rabbitMqManager)
{
    rabbitMqManager.call(new ChannelCallable<Void>()
    {
        @Override
        public String getDescription()
        {
            return "Declaring and binding: " +
                AUTHENTICATION_SERVICE_QUEUE;
        }

        @Override
        public Void call(final Channel channel) throws IOException
        {
            channel.exchangeDeclare(INTERNAL_SERVICES_EXCHANGE,
                "headers",
                true, // durable
                false, // auto-delete
                null); // arguments

            channel.queueDeclare(AUTHENTICATION_SERVICE_QUEUE,
                false, // durable
                false, // exclusive,
                true, // auto-delete
                null); // arguments
```

```
String routingKey = "";
Map<String, Object> arguments = new HashMap<>();
arguments.put("x-match", "all");
arguments.put("request_type", "login");
arguments.put("request_version", "v1");
channel.queueBind(AUTHENTICATION_SERVICE_QUEUE,
    INTERNAL_SERVICES_EXCHANGE, routingKey,
    arguments);

// other arguments unchanged
arguments.put("request_type", "logout");
channel.queueBind(AUTHENTICATION_SERVICE_QUEUE,
INTERNAL_SERVICES_EXCHANGE, routingKey, arguments);

        return null;
    }
});
```

Let's review what you've just coded. Once again, we put `RabbitMqManager` to good use, as it encapsulates all the logic to deal with connection and channel management. Observe how the exchange type is set to `headers`. Also observe how the queue is nondurable and autodeletable. As we've explained earlier, since service interactions are synchronous and short lived, there's no reason to have request messages survive a RabbitMQ restart. The queue is not exclusive because all the Java application servers will consume it simultaneously.

The binding part of this code is where the interesting things happen. A headers exchange is configured via *arguments* and not a routing key. This is why the routing key is an empty string. The arguments themselves are a map of key values that define the matching rules with the incoming message headers. A specific key (`x-match`) is used to specify whether any or all of the other key-value pairs should match.

In your case, you want to match the key with the version `v1` of the `login` and `logout` types of messages. So, you've bound the `authentication-service` queue to the `internal-services` exchange twice as follows:

- Once with `x-match=all, request_type=login, request_version=v1`
- Once with `x-match=all, request_type=logout, request_version=v1`

Now, let's look at how you've created the consumer for the `authentication-service` queue, as shown in the following code:

```
rabbitMqManager.createSubscription(AUTHENTICATION_SERVICE_QUEUE, new
SubscriptionDeliverHandler()
{
    @Override
```

```
public void handleDelivery(final Channel channel,
                           final Envelope envelope,
                           final BasicProperties
                               requestProperties,
                           final byte[] requestBody)
{
    try
    {
        channel.basicAck(envelope.getDeliveryTag(), false);
    }
    catch (final IOException ioe)
    {
        LOGGER.severe("Failed to acknowledge: "
                + reflectionToString(envelope,
                    SHORT_PREFIX_STYLE));
    }

    if (isBlank(requestProperties.getReplyTo()))
    {
        LOGGER.warning("Received request without reply-to: "
                + reflectionToString(envelope,
                    SHORT_PREFIX_STYLE));
        return;
    }

    handleRequest(channel, envelope, requestProperties,
        requestBody);
}
```

You shouldn't be surprised to see the re-use of the subscription mechanism that you created earlier. Since it deals with graceful reconnection, it's the right thing to do. Note how the incoming messages are acknowledged right away. It would make no sense to reject and redeliver a message in the context of a service-oriented request-response interaction. Thus, all messages are acknowledged independently, irrespective of what happens when handling them.

> The RabbitMQ Java SDK contains helper classes to create RPC clients and servers, including those with JSON-serialized messages. Consider using them, but make sure you understand their behavior in case of disconnection and agree with the message semantics they use.

The next method to look at is the one in charge of deserializing and dispatching the JSON messages to the actual methods. Let's take a look at the following code:

```
private void handleRequest(final Channel channel,
                           final Envelope envelope,
                           final BasicProperties
                               requestProperties,
                           final byte[] requestBody)
{
    try
    {
        final String contentEncoding =
            requestProperties.getContentEncoding();

        switch (requestProperties.getContentType())
        {
            case LOGIN_REQUEST_V1_CONTENT_TYPE :
            {
                final LoginRequestV1 request =
                    OBJECT_MAPPER.readValue(new
                    String(requestBody,
                    contentEncoding), LoginRequestV1.class);
                final LoginResponseV1 response = login(request);
                final byte[] responseBody =
                    OBJECT_MAPPER.writeValueAsString(response).
                    getBytes(
                    MESSAGE_ENCODING);
                respond(channel, requestProperties,
                    LOGIN_RESPONSE_V1_CONTENT_TYPE, responseBody);
                break;
            }

            case LOGOUT_REQUEST_V1_CONTENT_TYPE :
            {
                final LogoutRequestV1 request = OBJECT_MAPPER.
readValue(new String(requestBody,
                    contentEncoding), LogoutRequestV1.class);
                final LogoutResponseV1 response = logout(request);
                final byte[] responseBody = OBJECT_MAPPER.
writeValueAsString(response).getBytes(
                    MESSAGE_ENCODING);
                respond(channel, requestProperties, LOGOUT_RESPONSE_
V1_CONTENT_TYPE, responseBody);
                break;
            }
```

```
            default :
                throw new IllegalArgumentException("Unsupported
    message type: " + requestProperties.getContentType());
            }
        }
        catch (final Exception e)
        {
            handleException(channel, envelope, requestProperties, e);
        }
    }
}
```

As you can see, the dispatching mechanism is based on the message **content-type** property. Looking at this, three questions are certainly going to pop up in your head:

- Why not use the content-type property in the matching rule of the headers exchange? The answer is that it's just impossible, as matching rules only apply to custom message headers and not to any of the built-in message properties.

- Why not use the request_type and request_version headers in the switch expression? It's possible, but for this, we would need to concatenate them in a string that would end up being a variation of the content-type.

- Why not peek in the message content itself to find out its type? If we are using XML instead of JSON, we would use specific namespaces for that matter. JSON doesn't support that notion. One could argue that we could use a $schema property in our JSON payload and switch to it, but at the end of the day, we'd rather tell message types apart without having to parse them.

Observe that we also specifically deal with unsupported message types. The last thing we want is to silently swallow such messages. Instead, we want to make it clear to the developers and the operation team that something is not right with the system. On the other hand, valid request messages are deserialized to an object that gets passed to either the login or logout methods (which we won't detail here as their implementation is not directly relevant to our discussion).

Be strict and deserialize request and response JSON messages straight to objects with internal services. Different version numbers will allow you to evolve gracefully. Conversely, if you expose public services over AMQP, be lax with the request messages (do not bind them to objects), but stay strict with your response messages (serialize them from objects). This will cut some slack for external users who may lack the discipline or understanding needed when rigorously dealing with schema versions.

The objects returned from these methods are then sent to the reply queue using the `respond` method, which is listed in the following code with the important lines highlighted:

```
private void respond(final Channel channel,
                     final BasicProperties requestProperties,
                     final String responseContentType,
                     final byte[] responseBody) throws IOException
{
    final String messageId = UUID.randomUUID().toString();

    final BasicProperties props = new BasicProperties.Builder()
        .contentType(responseContentType)
        .contentEncoding(MESSAGE_ENCODING)
        .messageId(messageId)
        .correlationId(requestProperties.getCorrelationId())
        .deliveryMode(1)
        .build();

    channel.basicPublish("", requestProperties.getReplyTo(),
        props, responseBody);
}
```

The notable aspects of the `respond` method are as follows:

- The **correlation-id** of the request message is propagated to the response message. Though this is not required in your case, since you'll be using temporary reply queues, it is a good practice to do so. Moreover, it opens the door to switch to a permanent response queue should performance issues arise with the short-lived queues.

- The **delivery-mode** is set to 1, which indicates nonpersistence. Once again, this is because of the transient nature of request-response interactions.

- The response is published to the default exchange, the name of which is an empty string. The routing key used for the publication is the name of the reply queue, which is stored in the reply-to property for the request message.

Finally, let's take a look at the `handleException` method, which is called whenever anything goes wrong while handling a request message, whether this is done because the request message can't be deserialized, its type is unknown, or if the actual method being called ends up throwing an exception. This is shown in the following code:

```
private void handleException(final Channel channel,
                             final Envelope envelope,
                             final BasicProperties
                                 requestProperties,
```

```
                                         final Exception e1)
{
    LOGGER.log(SEVERE, "Failed to handle: " +
        reflectionToString(envelope, SHORT_PREFIX_STYLE),
        e1);

    try
    {
        final ErrorV1 error = new ErrorV1()
            .withContext( reflectionToString(envelope,
                SHORT_PREFIX_STYLE))
            .withMessage(e1.getMessage());
        final byte[] responseBody =
            OBJECT_MAPPER.writeValueAsString(error).getBytes(
            MESSAGE_ENCODING);
        respond(channel, requestProperties, ERROR_V1_CONTENT_TYPE,
            responseBody);
    }
    catch (final Exception e2)
    {
        LOGGER.log(SEVERE,
            "Failed to respond error for: " +
                reflectionToString(envelope, SHORT_PREFIX_STYLE),
            e2);
    }
}
```

Observe how a generic error message is used as the service response when an exception occurs. This is a very simple and powerful way of propagating potential issues back to the caller of a message-oriented service. Since this is an internal service, it is perfectly fine if the error message carries lots of contextual information.

You're done with the implementation of the authentication service. After deploying the preceding code, the internal-services exchange and the authentication-service queue is created. By looking at the bindings of the latter in the management console, you can visually confirm that the correct bindings and headers that match the specified rules are in place, as shown in the following screenshot:

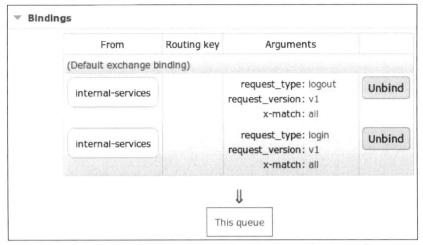

The routing and matching rules of a queue bound twice to a headers exchange

Now that the service is ready, it's time to write a client that interacts with it.

Calling the authentication service

If you remember the initial use case, CCM wants to interact with the authentication service from the Ruby-on-Rails back office application. Therefore, you will implement the client in Ruby. The code you came up with is reproduced as follows:

```ruby
channel   = AMQP::Channel.new(connection)

channel.on_error do |ch, channel_close|
  connection.close { EventMachine.stop }
  raise "Channel error: #{channel_close.inspect()}"
end

channel.headers(
      'internal-services',
      :durable     => true,
      :auto_delete => false,
      :passive     => true) do |exchange|

  channel.queue('',
    :exclusive => true,
    :durable => false,
    :auto_delete => true) do |response_queue|

    response_queue.subscribe do |metadata, payload|
      handle_response(metadata.content_type, payload)
    end

    puts "Response queue created: #{response_queue.name}"
```

```
      message_id = SecureRandom.uuid
      message_json = JSON.generate({
        :username => user_name,
        :password => password})

      exchange.publish(
        message_json,
        :content_type      => 'application/vnd.ccm.login.req.v1+json',
        :content_encoding  => 'UTF-8',
        :message_id        => message_id,
        :correlation_id    => message_id,
        :reply_to          => response_queue.name,
        :headers           => { :request_type => 'login',
                                :request_version => 'v1' })
    end

    EventMachine.add_timer(3) do
      puts 'No response after 3 seconds'
      connection.close { EventMachine.stop }
    end
  end
end
```

There are several interesting bits in this code. Observe that first, a *passive* declaration of the `internal-services` headers exchange is performed. What does this mean? Basically, it is a declaration attempt that just checks the existence of the exchange, the expected routing type, and the durability configuration. If you remember our discussion about **check then act** strategies in *Chapter 2, Creating an Application Inbox*, you're probably thinking "Ah hah! You're doing the opposite of what you preached." Actually, in this case, it's okay if the exchange gets deleted after the check and the subsequent publish operation fails; the failure will be dealt with by the channel error handler (at the top of the code snippet). This passive declaration saves you the effort of creating a temporary queue for no reason if it's clear that the publish operation will fail anyway.

With this in place, the next step consists of creating the exclusive autodelete response queue. Did you spot that an empty string is used for its name? This means that it will be up to RabbitMQ to generate a unique name for the queue, which is what you want since you're using short-lived response queues. Then, the response handler gets subscribed to the queue, which makes sense because we want to do this before sending the request. Otherwise, we may not be ready to receive the response if it comes back very quickly.

After this, the login message is created and published to the exchange with the necessary `reply_to` property and the `request_type` and `request_version` headers. For good measure, a `correlation_id` property is also provided, though it's not used since a temporary queue is used for the response (instead of a permanent one).

 You can learn more about EventMachine and how it enables Ruby to execute a code in a nonblocking fashion at `http://rubyeventmachine.com`.

Finally, a time-out is set in order to deal with a case where no service response comes back. This is crucial if you do not want to block the client application threads forever in case there is an issue with the service, a blocking that could eventually make the whole application unusable.

 Reasonable time-outs is one of the secret sauces of distributed systems that degrade gracefully when things go haywire. Another ingredient of the secret sauce is retries with exponential back-offs and a capped number of attempts.

You're done with the authentication service client. If you glance at the management console while a service request is underway, you will see the temporary reply queue right above the `authentication-service` queue, as illustrated in the following screenshot. The name of the management console starts with `amq.gen-` to make it clear that it's a name that has been generated by RabbitMQ. Observe that the queue is exclusively accessible to its owner:

A transient reply queue and the authentication service queue involved in a request-response interaction

At this point, you've built a solid message-oriented SOA foundation that you build upon to roll out new services or new versions of existing services as the need arises.

Summary

In this chapter, you learned the principles of performing service invocations in a message-oriented manner. You learned how to roll out services and clients and configure RabbitMQ to smartly route messages back and forth between them.

By now, all the features Clever Coney Media was planning to implement on RabbitMQ are established. It's now time to turn your attention to the operational aspects of RabbitMQ in production. That's what the next chapter of this book will focus on.

7
Taking RabbitMQ to Production

Who wants to have all their eggs in the same basket? No one of course, but this is basically what Clever Coney Media has been doing so far since it has been running a single instance of RabbitMQ in production. In this chapter, you'll learn how to address this concern using the clustering and federation features of RabbitMQ. You'll also learn how to check the pulse of the brokers and get alerts if things start turning sour.

In this chapter, you will learn about:

- Broker clustering
- High-availability queues
- The federation plug cluster in
- Monitoring RabbitMQ

Tackling the broker SPOF

So far, Clever Coney Media has been running a single instance of RabbitMQ for all its production needs. Things have been running smoothly, but it's just a matter of time until something bad happens. Though RabbitMQ brokers are extremely stable, a crash is always possible. Losing an instance altogether due to a virtual instance glitch is a likely possibility that can't be ignored if you're running in the cloud. Therefore, it is essential to tackle the broker **single point of failure** (**SPOF**) before something bad happens, to prevent losing data, annoying users, and avoiding the dreaded 2 a.m. phone calls.

The good news is that RabbitMQ provides all the necessary features to deal with this issue out of the box. Indeed, RabbitMQ can easily be configured to run in an **active/active** deployment, where several brokers are engaged in a cluster to act as a single highly-available AMQP middleware. The active/active aspect is essential, because it means that no manual **fail-over** operation is needed if one broker goes down, again sparing you a 2 a.m. phone call.

Therefore CCM decides to roll out a second RabbitMQ broker (named `rmq-prod-2`) and cluster it with the one it already has (named `rmq-prod-1`). This would lead to the architecture represented in the following diagram:

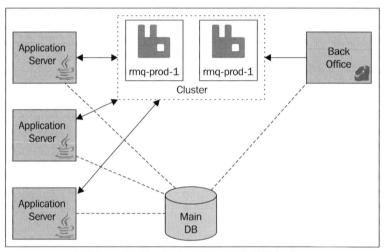

A high-availability cluster of two RabbitMQ brokers

CCM informs you when the second instance of RabbitMQ is ready that needs to be clustered with the already existing one. It has made sure that the content of the file in `/var/lib/rabbitmq/.erlang.cookie` is the same as in the first instance. This is required because RabbitMQ relies on Erlang's clustering feature, which allows several Erlang nodes to communicate with each other locally or over the network. The Erlang cluster requires a so-called **security cookie** as a means of cross-node authentication.

If your RabbitMQ instances are firewalled from each other, you'll need to open specific ports on top of the one used by AMQP (5672); otherwise, the cluster will not work. You can get more information at `http://www.rabbitmq.com/clustering.html#firewall`.

You do not need to configure any user or virtual host on the second node, like you did in *Chapter 1, A Rabbit Springs to Life*. Instead, you just have to join the cluster, and its configuration will automatically be synchronized with the existing RabbitMQ instance, including users, virtual hosts, exchanges, queues, and policies.

> Keep in mind that when a node joins a cluster, it will be completely reset. All its configuration and data will be deleted before it synchronizes with the other members of the cluster.

For this, you run the following command on the second node:

```
$ sudo rabbitmqctl stop_app
Stopping node rabbit@rmq-prod-2 ...
...done.
$ sudo rabbitmqctl join_cluster rabbit@rmq-prod-1
Clustering node rabbit@rmq-prod-2 with rabbit@rmq-prod-1 ...
...done.
$ sudo rabbitmqctl start_app
Starting node rabbit@rmq-prod-2 ...
...done.
```

> Make sure the same version of Erlang is used by all the RabbitMQ nodes that engage in a cluster; otherwise, the join_cluster command will fail with an OTP version mismatch error.
>
> Similarly, the same major/minor version of RabbitMQ should be used across nodes, but patch versions can differ; this means that versions 3.2.1 and 3.2.0 can be used in the same cluster, but not 3.2.1 and 3.1.0.

After running these commands, you can check whether the cluster is active by running the cluster_status command on any node. Hereafter, you run it on the first node:

```
$ sudo rabbitmqctl cluster_status
Cluster status of node rabbit@rmq-prod-1 ...
[{nodes,[{disc,[rabbit@rmq-prod-2,rabbit@rmq-prod-1]}]},
 {running_nodes,[rabbit@rmq-prod-2,rabbit@rmq-prod-1]},
 {partitions,[]}]
...done.
```

Notice how two lists of nodes are given in the status message: the one named `nodes` is the list of configured nodes in the cluster, while the one named `running_nodes` lists the nodes that are actually active. The list of configured nodes is persistent, so it will survive a restart of the brokers. On restart, each broker will automatically re-engage with the cluster.

Spend some time getting acquainted with RabbitMQ's behavior in a split-brain (also known as network partition) situation at `http://www.rabbitmq.com/partitions.html`.

We've said that the entire configuration will be synchronized on the new node joining the cluster. You can confirm this by connecting to the management console on the second node. You can use the `ccm-admin` user to log in because it's been synchronized. As you can see in the following screenshot of the **Queues** view of the management console, the configuration has actually been synchronized:

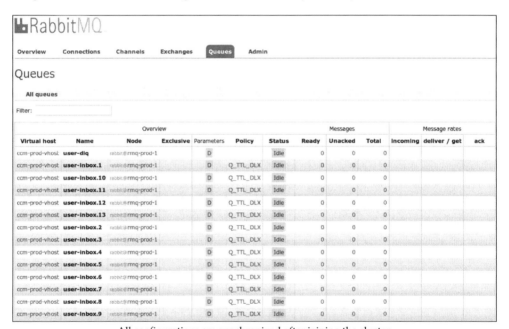

All configurations are synchronized after joining the cluster

If you want to add more nodes, you would only need to have each new node join one of the other nodes in the cluster. It would then discover all the other nodes in the cluster automatically (a neat feature provided by the underlying Erlang clustering mechanism).

In the management console of the first node, the **Overview** tab shows all the nodes that are in the cluster, as illustrated in the following screenshot:

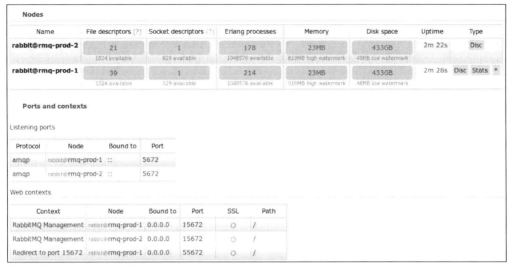

Nodes							
Name	File descriptors (?)	Socket descriptors (?)	Erlang processes	Memory	Disk space	Uptime	Type
rabbit@rmq-prod-2	21 1024 available	1 829 available	178 1048576 available	23MB 819MB high watermark	433GB 48MB low watermark	2m 22s	Disc
rabbit@rmq-prod-1	39 1024 available	1 829 available	214 1048576 available	23MB 819MB high watermark	433GB 48MB low watermark	2m 28s	Disc Stats *

Ports and contexts

Listening ports

Protocol	Node	Bound to	Port
amqp	rabbit@rmq-prod-1 ::		5672
amqp	rabbit@rmq-prod-2 ::		5672

Web contexts

Context	Node	Bound to	Port	SSL	Path
RabbitMQ Management	rabbit@rmq-prod-1	0.0.0.0	15672	○	/
RabbitMQ Management	rabbit@rmq-prod-2	0.0.0.0	15672	○	/
Redirect to port 15672	rabbit@rmq-prod-1	0.0.0.0	55672	○	/

The management console overview shows all cluster members

As you can see, all the members of the cluster are listed, including the statistics and ports they've opened (both for AMQP and the management console itself). You may be wondering what the different values shown in the **Type** column are. **Disc** means that this node persists its data to the filesystem, which is the default behavior. It's also possible to start a node as a **ram node**, in which case all message data will be purely stored in memory. This is an interesting approach for creating high-performance members in a cluster. **Stats** means the node is the one that contains the management statistics database, which is not spread across the cluster. Finally, the * indicates the node you're connected to.

 Nodes can be removed from the cluster, as explained in this tutorial at `http://www.rabbitmq.com/clustering.html#breakup`.

At this point, you're probably thinking you're done with clustering. In fact, there's one more step to perform to ensure the high availability of your queues' data.

Mirroring queues

With clustering, you ensured that the configuration gets synchronized across all RabbitMQ nodes. This means that clients can now connect to one node or the other and find the exchanges and queues they're expecting. However, there is one thing that is not carried over the cluster by default: the messages themselves. By default, queue data is local to a particular node; so if this node goes down, consumers will have to wait until it comes back to access it. This may sound strange, but it can be a perfectly acceptable scenario for messages used to track long running tasks, for example, for which having to wait for a while would not be tragic.

In your case, you want the data in the users' queues to be highly available. This can be achieved with **mirrored queues**. When a queue is mirrored, its instances across the network organize themselves around one master and several slaves. All interaction (message queuing and dequeuing) happens with the master; the slaves receive the updates via synchronization over the cluster. If you interact with a node that hosts a slave queue, the interaction would actually be forwarded across the cluster to the master and then synchronized back to the slave.

Activating queue mirroring is done via a policy that is applied to each queue concerned. Since only one policy at a time is allowed on a queue (or exchange), you will first have to clear the Q_TTL_DLX policy you created in *Chapter 5, Tweaking Message Delivery* and apply a new policy that composes the Q_TTL_DLX policy with the queue mirroring one (that is, the high-availability queue). This sounds more complicated than it is, as you can see by running the following command:

```
$ sudo rabbitmqctl clear_policy -p ccm-prod-vhost Q_TTL_DLX

Clearing policy "Q_TTL_DLX" ...

...done.

$ sudo rabbitmqctl set_policy -p ccm-prod-vhost HA_Q_TTL_DLX "user-
  .+" '{"message-ttl":604800000, "dead-letter-exchange":"user-dlx",
  "ha-mode":"all", "ha-sync-mode":"automatic"}' --apply-to queues

  Setting policy "HA_Q_TTL_DLX" for pattern "user-.+" to "{\"ha-
  mode\":\"all\", \"message-ttl\":604800000, \"dead-letter-
  exchange\":\"user-dlx\"}" with priority "0" ...

...done.
```

As you can see, you just added "ha-mode":"all" to the existing TTL and DLX policy rules. The all value for ha-mode means that the queues will be mirrored across all nodes in the cluster, which is exactly what you want for your two-node cluster. Other options are exactly and nodes, which allow specifying a number or nodes and a list of node names in an extra ha-params parameter respectively.

The `ha-sync-mode` parameter is unsurprisingly used to specify the synchronization mode for the mirrored queue, and can be either `manual` or `automatic`. In the manual mode, a newly mirrored slave queue will not receive any of the existing messages, but will eventually become consistent with the master queue, as old messages get consumed. In your case, you want immediate synchronization of the queues so that any existing messages become visible across all nodes, and are fine with the initial unresponsiveness this will create, as performance is not critical for user messages.

It is possible to manually synchronize a mirrored queue with `rabbitmqctl sync_queue <queue_name>`. The manual synchronization can be canceled with `rabbitmqctl cancel_sync_ queue <queue_name>`.

You certainly must have noticed that we apply this policy only to the user inboxes and dead-letter queue. You're most likely wondering about the log and the service queues. For the log queues, we will be looking at another high-availability option because it does not make sense to mirror the high traffic that goes through them across the cluster. For the service temporary response queues, there is no need to make them highly available; if something goes wrong with a broker, the synchronous interaction will break and the client will have to back off and retry. However, the service request queues need to be mirrored to allow providers and consumers to be connected to different RabbitMQ brokers. This is done with the following command:

```
$ sudo rabbitmqctl set_policy -p ccm-prod-vhost HA_Q ".+-service" '{"ha-
mode":"all", "ha-sync-mode":"automatic"}' --apply-to queuesSetting policy
"HA_Q" for pattern ".+-service" to "{\"ha-mode\":\"all\", \"ha-sync-
mode\":\"automatic\"}" with priority "0" ...

...done.
```

As you can see, you opted for the `.+-service` pattern, so any new service that you could develop alongside the authentication one will have its request queue automatically mirrored, as long as its name ends with `-service`.

If you take a look at the **Queues** tab of the management console after running the above command, you'll see that the **HA_Q_TTL_DLX** and **HA_Q** policies have been applied to the intended queues, as visible in the following screenshot:

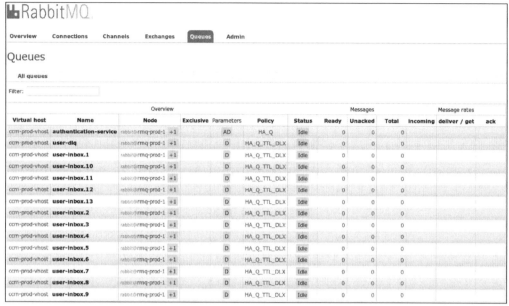

					Overview				Messages			Message rates	
Virtual host	Name	Node	Exclusive	Parameters	Policy	Status	Ready	Unacked	Total	Incoming	deliver / get	ack
ccm-prod-vhost	authentication-service	rabbit@rmq-prod-1 +1	AD		HA_Q	Idle	0	0	0			
ccm-prod-vhost	user-dlq	rabbit@rmq-prod-1 +1	D		HA_Q_TTL_DLX	Idle	0	0	0			
ccm-prod-vhost	user-inbox.1	rabbit@rmq-prod-1 +1	D		HA_Q_TTL_DLX	Idle	0	0	0			
ccm-prod-vhost	user-inbox.10	rabbit@rmq-prod-1 +1	D		HA_Q_TTL_DLX	Idle	0	0	0			
ccm-prod-vhost	user-inbox.11	rabbit@rmq-prod-1 +1	D		HA_Q_TTL_DLX	Idle	0	0	0			
ccm-prod-vhost	user-inbox.12	rabbit@rmq-prod-1 +1	D		HA_Q_TTL_DLX	Idle	0	0	0			
ccm-prod-vhost	user-inbox.13	rabbit@rmq-prod-1 +1	D		HA_Q_TTL_DLX	Idle	0	0	0			
ccm-prod-vhost	user-inbox.2	rabbit@rmq-prod-1 +1	D		HA_Q_TTL_DLX	Idle	0	0	0			
ccm-prod-vhost	user-inbox.3	rabbit@rmq-prod-1 +1	D		HA_Q_TTL_DLX	Idle	0	0	0			
ccm-prod-vhost	user-inbox.4	rabbit@rmq-prod-1 +1	D		HA_Q_TTL_DLX	Idle	0	0	0			
ccm-prod-vhost	user-inbox.5	rabbit@rmq-prod-1 +1	D		HA_Q_TTL_DLX	Idle	0	0	0			
ccm-prod-vhost	user-inbox.6	rabbit@rmq-prod-1 +1	D		HA_Q_TTL_DLX	Idle	0	0	0			
ccm-prod-vhost	user-inbox.7	rabbit@rmq-prod-1 +1	D		HA_Q_TTL_DLX	Idle	0	0	0			
ccm-prod-vhost	user-inbox.8	rabbit@rmq-prod-1 +1	D		HA_Q_TTL_DLX	Idle	0	0	0			
ccm-prod-vhost	user-inbox.9	rabbit@rmq-prod-1 +1	D		HA_Q_TTL_DLX	Idle	0	0	0			

Mirrored queues with the HA policies applied.

Notice how the mirrored queues have a **+1** next to them. It's not an option for sharing them with your friends on Google Plus; instead, it denotes the fact that the queues are mirrored to one other node in the cluster. Staying in the management console, if you look at **Details** of any mirrored queue, you will see something similar to the next image. As you can see, the master node (**rabbit@rmq-prod-1**) and the slave nodes (only **rabbit@rmq-prod-2**, in your case) are clearly detailed:

Master and slave nodes are detailed for each mirrored queue

At this point, the RabbitMQ brokers are clustered and user queues are mirrored. However, the client applications are not yet able to benefit from this highly-available deployment. Let's fix this right away.

Connecting to the cluster

The applications that connect to RabbitMQ need to be modified a little so that they can benefit from the cluster. Currently, they connect to a single node and thus, should be modified to be able to connect to both nodes, trying one and failing over to the other one in case of trouble. Besides this modification, no other change is required from the client applications. They will continue to interact with the exchanges and queues they know about in the same way as before.

Let's first modify the main Java application. All you need to do is edit the `RabbitMqManager` class, so it receives by injection both a `com.rabbitmq.client.ConnectionFactory` and an array of `com.rabbitmq.client.Address` instances, one for each RabbitMQ node. Then you can modify the `start()` method as shown in the following code:

```
public void start()
{
    try
    {
        connection = factory.newConnection(addresses);
        connection.addShutdownListener(this);
        LOGGER.info("Connected to " + connection.getAddress().
getHostName() + ":" + connection.getPort());
        restartSubscriptions();
    }
    catch (final Exception e)
    {
        LOGGER.log(Level.SEVERE, "Failed to connect to " + Arrays.
toString(addresses), e);
        asyncWaitAndReconnect();
    }
}
```

Basically, the list of broker addresses is passed to the connection factory and the actual connection is used in the success log statement, while the list of addresses is used in the failure log statement. With this in place, the RabbitMQ Java client will connect to the first responsive node in the address list and will try each of the provided broker addresses until it can establish a connection, or eventually fail. In case of failure, the overall reconnect mechanism you've already put in place will kick in and the addresses will once again be attempted for connection. The following code illustrates how `connection factory` and the list of addresses are created before being passed on to `RabbitMqManager`:

```
ConnectionFactory factory = new ConnectionFactory();
factory.setUsername("ccm-prod");
```

```
factory.setPassword("******");
factory.setVirtualHost("ccm-prod-vhost");

Address[] addresses = new Address[]{
    new Address("rmq-prod-1", 5672),
    new Address("rmq-prod-2", 5672)};
```

With this in place, the main Java application is able to benefit from the cluster. Let's turn our attention to the Ruby on Rails back office. Things are a little simpler here because it doesn't maintain a permanent connection to RabbitMQ. Therefore, all that is needed is a mechanism to attempt connecting to the first broker, then the second, and run a block provided on the first successfully established connection.

You can achieve this very elegantly, thanks to the on_tcp_connection_failure mechanism provided by the amqp gem, as follows:

```
def run_with_connection(settings, &action)
  broker = settings[:brokers].shift

  raise "Impossible to connect to any broker" if broker.nil?

  settings.merge!(broker)

  settings.merge!({
    :on_tcp_connection_failure => Proc.new {
      run_with_connection(settings, &action)
    }
  })

  EventMachine.run do
    AMQP.connect(settings) do |connection|
      action.call(connection)
    end
  end
end

settings = {
  :brokers  => [
                 {:host => 'rmq-prod-1', :port=> 5672},
                 {:host => 'rmq-prod-2', :port=> 5672}
               ],
  :vhost    => "ccm-prod-vhost",
  :user     => "ccm-prod",
  :password => "******"
}
```

Notice how each connection is attempted by mutating the settings hash using the broker host and port information. With this in place, calling `run_with_connection(settings)` will create a valid connection to RabbitMQ and pass it to the block provided.

At this point, you've taken care of all the systems concerned with user queues. But what about the log aggregation mechanism? It's indeed time to address this concern.

Federating brokers

So far, you've followed an approach to high availability that most developers should be very familiar with. The way you created a cluster of two RabbitMQ brokers is really similar to what is typically done when making a relational database highly available. The database remains a centralized resource that offers high guarantees of availability. But RabbitMQ is not a one-trick rabbit when it comes to high availability. Remember, you left the log queues out of the equation for a reason; you did not want to mirror such a highly-trafficked queue. What could you do in order for CCM to enjoy the same guarantees for log aggregation? Enter the notion of **messaging topologies**.

If you think beyond the notion of a single centralized enterprise resource and instead think in terms of distributed components, the idea of creating a topology of RabbitMQ brokers will emerge. RabbitMQ offers the following two plugins that allow the connection of brokers:

- The **shovel** plugin, which connects queues in one broker to exchanges in another broker
- The **federation** plugin, which connects queues to queues or exchanges to exchanges across brokers

Both plugins ensure a reliable delivery of messages across brokers; if messages can't be routed to the target broker, they'll remain safely accumulated. Neither require brokers to be clustered, which simplifies setup and management (RabbitMQ and Erlang versions can mismatch). Moreover, both plugins work fine over WAN connections, something clustering doesn't do well.

 In a federation, only the node where messages converge needs to be manually configured; its upstream nodes get automatically configured for the topology. Conversely with shovels, each source node needs to be manually configured to send to a destination node, which itself is unaware of the fact that it's engaged in a particular topology.

In your case, the ideal topology consists of running a RabbitMQ node collocated with each application that emits logs to the app-logs topic exchange (refer to *Chapter 4, Handling Application Logs*), and have this exchange forward all messages to a centralized single RabbitMQ node where the app-logs-archiver and app-logs-error-reporter queues will be bound. This topology is illustrated in the following diagram:

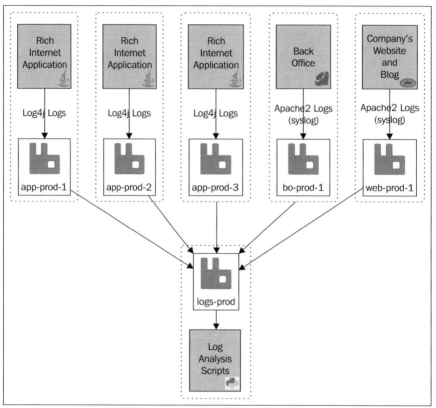

A topology that federates log messages to a central broker

In this topology, all applications will write to a local RabbitMQ node, which will act as a store-and-forward broker, pushing all logs to a centralized RabbitMQ node. If this central node is down, the log entries will remain locally accumulated until it comes back up. Obviously, the assumption here is that the local RabbitMQ nodes are extremely stable. Your experience with running RabbitMQ in the past few months will help you with this approach. Moreover, logs are considered important but not critical data for CCM, so a best-effort approach is acceptable. Knowing this, you chose to use the federation plugin, as it's the one that supports exchange to exchange connectivity (with shovel, messages would have to be accumulated in a local queue on each node).

More information on the shovel plugin can be found at
`http://www.rabbitmq.com/shovel.html`.

The federation plugin needs to be installed on all RabbitMQ nodes that will engage in the topology. Therefore, you install it by running the following commands on each node:

```
$ sudo rabbitmq-plugins enable rabbitmq_federation

The following plugins have been enabled:

  rabbitmq_federation

Plugin configuration has changed. Restart RabbitMQ for changes to take
effect.
$ sudo rabbitmq-plugins enable rabbitmq_federation_management

The following plugins have been enabled:

  rabbitmq_federation_management

Plugin configuration has changed. Restart RabbitMQ for changes to take
effect.
```

Moreover, unlike with clustering, each node needs to be manually set up to have the desired user and virtual host configured. Therefore, you need to run the necessary command, as discussed in *Chapter 1, A Rabbit Springs to Life*. Next, you need to configure the `apps-log` exchange federation itself. This involves multiple steps (which we will detail hereafter) that are all run on the central broker, that is, the one towards which all logs will converge. First, you need to configure what are called **upstreams**, which are the RabbitMQ nodes that will send data to the central broker.

Five upstreams are needed, since there are five servers that will send logs over; however, we will only consider two in the following examples for brevity's sake. What you're about to do for two upstreams will be done the same way for the other three:

```
$ sudo rabbitmqctl set_parameter -p ccm-prod-vhost federation-upstream
app-prod-1-logs '{"uri":"amqp://ccm-prod:******@app-prod-1:5672/ccm-prod-
vhost"}'

Setting runtime parameter "app-prod-1-logs" for component "federation-
upstream" to "{\"uri\":\"amqp://ccm-prod:******@app-prod-1:5672/ccm-prod-
vhost\"}" ...

...done.

$ sudo rabbitmqctl set_parameter -p ccm-prod-vhost federation-upstream
app-prod-2-logs '{"uri":"amqp://ccm-prod:******@app-prod-2:5672/ccm-prod-
vhost"}'
```

```
Setting runtime parameter "app-prod-2-logs" for component "federation-
upstream" to "{\"uri\":\"amqp://ccm-prod:******@app-prod-2:5672/ccm-prod-
vhost\"}" ...
```

```
...done.
```

The next step consists of creating an upstream set, which is a logical group of upstreams referred to by their names. You run the following command to create an upstream set named app-prod-logs, and that contains the app-prod-1-logs and app-prod-2-logs upstreams:

```
$ sudo rabbitmqctl set_parameter -p ccm-prod-vhost federation-upstream-
set app-prod-logs '[{"upstream": "app-prod-1-logs"},{"upstream": "app-
prod-2-logs"}]'
```

```
Setting runtime parameter "app-prod-logs" for component "federation-
upstream-set" to "[{\"upstream\": \"app-prod-1-logs\"},{\"upstream\":
\"app-prod-2-logs\"}]" ...
```

```
...done.
```

> If you know that you'll never have more than one logical group of upstreams, you can skip the creation of an upstream set and use the implicit set named all, which automatically contains all the upstreams in a virtual host.

After this, you need to configure the user that the federation plugin will use in the central broker to interact with the federated exchange, with the following command:

```
$ sudo rabbitmqctl set_parameter federation local-username '"ccm-
  prod"'
```

```
Setting runtime parameter "local-username" for component "federation"
  to "\"ccm-prod\"" ...
```

```
...done.
```

If you browse the **Federation Upstreams** tab in the **Admin** section of the management console, you'll see that the two upstreams have been correctly configured (as shown in the following screenshot):

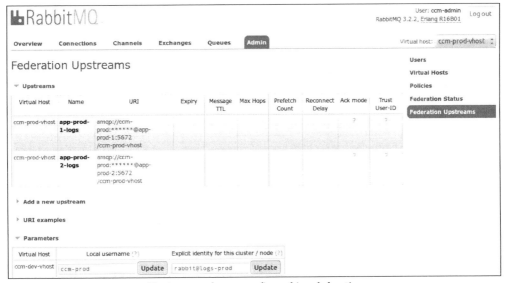

Upstream nodes are configured in a federation

If you switch to **Federation Status**, you'll see that it's empty, meaning that it's inactive. Why is that? After all, you've just created the topology. The reason is no exchange nor is queue yet actively engaged in the topology. Because of its dynamic nature, the federation is inactive. To bring it to life, you need to create a policy applied to the app-logs exchange that configures it to be federated with the app-prod-logs upstream set you've just created. You decide on naming this policy LOGS_UPSTREAM and run the following command:

```
$ sudo rabbitmqctl set_policy -p ccm-prod-vhost --apply-to exchanges
  LOGS_UPSTREAM "app-logs" '{"federation-upstream-set":"app-prod-
  logs"}'
Setting policy "LOGS_UPSTREAM" for pattern "app-logs" to
  "{\"federation-upstream-set\":\"app-prod-logs\"}" with priority "0" ...
...done.
```

After running this command, if you come back to the **Federation Status** tab, you'll see that the federation is now running links for the **app-logs** exchange from the two upstream nodes of the configured set (as shown in the following screenshot):

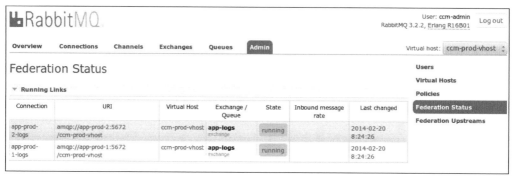

Running upstream links for a federated exchange

If you look at the **app-logs** exchange on this node, you'll see that there's nothing special to it, except that it has the **LOGS_UPSTREAM** policy applied to it (as represented in the following screenshot):

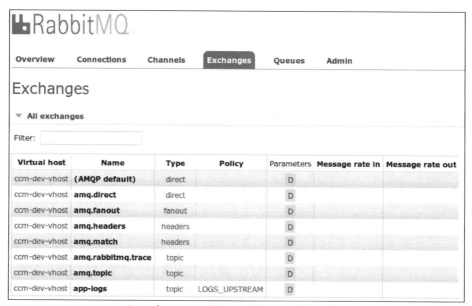

An exchange gets federated via a specific policy

 It's also possible to get the status of the federation from the command line by running `sudo rabbitmqctl eval 'rabbit_federation_ status:status().'` on the downstream node.

Now if you connect to the management console of any of the upstream nodes and look at the same exchange, you'll see what's represented in the following image. Now we're talking! The downstream node clearly has informed the upstream nodes of the federation, because the link established for the **app-logs** exchange is clearly visible (albeit grayed out, you may need to squint to be able to read it).

Virtual host	Name	Type	Policy	Parameters	Message rate in	Message rate out
ccm-dev-vhost	(AMQP default)	direct		D		
ccm-dev-vhost	amq.direct	direct		D		
ccm-dev-vhost	amq.fanout	fanout		D		
ccm-dev-vhost	amq.headers	headers		D		
ccm-dev-vhost	amq.match	headers		D		
ccm-dev-vhost	amq.rabbitmq.trace	topic		D		
ccm-dev-vhost	amq.topic	topic		D		
ccm-dev-vhost	app-logs	topic		D		
ccm-dev-vhost	federation: app-logs -> rabbit@logs-prod A	x-federation-upstream		D AD I Args		

In an upstream node, federation links are visible in the management console

If you look at the **Connections** and **Channels** tabs of the management console, you'll see that the downstream node is connected to the upstream mode over the AMQP protocol. Except for the setup of the topology itself, there's nothing magical about the federation. It's been built on top of AMQP, and thus, benefits from the same advantages offered by the protocol. Hence, if your RabbitMQ instances are firewalled, no special port besides the one used by AMQP (5672 by default) needs to be opened.

> You can read more about the federation plugin at http://www.rabbitmq.com/federation.html and http://www.rabbitmq.com/federation-reference.html.

From now on, you'll sleep better at night. You've clustered the nodes that were required to be highly available and deployed the others in a reliable topology. But what if things are going really bad with a broker? How will you know? It's time to review some monitoring strategies.

Monitoring the broker

The last task required to ensure a smooth production ride with RabbitMQ is the same as that of any other system; proper monitoring and alerting should be put in place in order to stay abreast of what's happening in the running brokers. In essence, the two questions you need to ask yourself are: what to monitor and how to monitor it? Let's take time to answer these two questions in the context of Clever Coney Media. We won't be discussing the monitoring of the machines (hardware or virtual) on which the brokers run, but will be focusing on the RabbitMQ specifics only.

Let's tackle the "how" first. There are two main ways to retrieve live information from a RabbitMQ broker: via the `rabbitmqctl` command-line tool and via the REST API exposed over HTTP by the management console. Any decent monitoring system will be able to use one or the other in order to collect metrics and report them to its central aggregation, charting, and alerting engine.

> An experimental SNMP monitoring plugin has been developed for RabbitMQ. I have successfully used it in the past, but its development has unfortunately been abandoned.

Since you've installed the management console at CCM, you're opting to use its rich and well-documented REST API over the command-line tool. The documentation of this API is available at `http://localhost:15672/api/` on any RabbitMQ node where the plugin is installed.

> Keep in mind that the management console is backed by the API, so anything you see and do with your browser can be done via the API.

CCM uses Zabbix as its monitoring tool of choice, so you'll be writing single-line shell commands to gather metrics locally and send them to the Zabbix server. All in all, the monitoring architecture will be as represented in the following diagram:

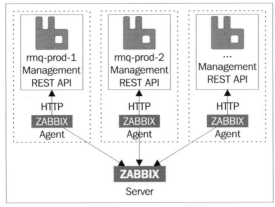

RabbitMQ monitoring architecture at CCM

 You can learn more about Zabbix by reading *Mastering Zabbix* from *Packt Publishing*. You can get more information at http://www. packtpub.com/monitor-large-information-technology- environment-by-using-zabbix/book.

Let's now detail the "what". Here are the different checks and metrics you've decided to implement and their related commands:

- **Node liveness**: Check whether RabbitMQ is performing its basic duties by executing a set of commands (declares the aliveness-test queue, publishes to, and consumes from it). Set the alarm to fire if the command returns 0 as follows:

```
curl -s http://ccm-admin:******@localhost:15672/api/aliveness-
  test/ccm-prod-vhost | grep -c "ok"
```

- **Cluster size**: Check on each of the clustered nodes their view of the active cluster size (it can differ in case of a network partition). Set the alarm to fire if the size is less than the healthy cluster size, which is 2 in your case, as follows:

```
curl -s http://ccm-admin:******@localhost:15672/api/nodes |
  grep -o "contexts" | wc -l
```

- **Federation status**: Check the active upstream links on the central log aggregation broker and raise an alarm if it's less than the optimal size (5 in your case) as follows:

```
curl -s http://ccm-admin:******@localhost:15672/api/
    federation-links/ccm-prod-vhost | grep -o "running" | wc -l
```

- **Queues high-watermarks**: Ensure the number of available messages in a queue is below a certain threshold. In your case, you'll verify that both the user-dlq and authentication-service queues have less than 25 messages in them. Otherwise, an alarm will be raised to indicate that either the consumers are down or are too slow and most of them would need to be provisioned. The scripts have to be written to fail gracefully if the queues don't exist:

```
curl -s -f http://ccm-admin:******@localhost:15672/api/queues/
    ccm-dev-vhost/user-dlq | jq '.messages_ready'
```

```
curl -s -f http://ccm-admin:******@localhost:15672/api/queues/
    ccm-dev-vhost/authentication-service | jq '.messages_ready'
```

- **Overall message throughput**: Monitor the intensity of the messaging traffic on a particular broker, for which you won't set any particular alarm (you may have to add an alarm if a throughput threshold proves to be the upper limit of what one of your broker can withstand). The following command will do the same for you:

```
curl -s http://ccm-admin:******@localhost:15672/api/vhosts/
    ccm-prod-vhost | jq '.messages_details.rate'
```

Some metrics come with related rigid upper limits whose values are also available from the API. For these, you'll raise an alarm whenever a threshold of 80 percent of the upper limit is reached. The following script will return false when the alarm must be raised. Let's detail them:

- **File descriptors**: The performance of the message persistence on the disk can be affected if not enough descriptors are available.

```
curl -s http://ccm-admin:******@localhost:15672/api/
    nodes/rabbit@${host} | jq '.fd_used<.fd_total*.8'
```

- **Socket descriptors**: RabbitMQ will stop accepting new connections if these descriptors are exhausted.

```
curl -s http://ccm-admin:******@localhost:15672/api/nodes/
rabbit@${host} | jq '.sockets_used<.sockets_total*.8'
```

- **Erlang processes**: There is an upper limit to the number of processes that can be created in an Erlang VM. Albeit if very high (around a million), it is worth keeping an eye on them.

```
curl -s http://ccm-admin:******@localhost:15672/api/nodes/
  rabbit@${host} | jq '.proc_used<.proc_total*.8'
```

- **Memory and disk space**: If any of these system resources get exhausted, RabbitMQ will not be able to work properly.

```
curl -s http://ccm-admin:******@localhost:15672/api/nodes/
rabbit@${host} | jq '.mem_used<.mem_limit*.8'
```

```
curl -s http://ccm-admin:******@localhost:15672/api/nodes/
rabbit@${host} | jq '.disk_free_limit<.disk_free*.8'
```

On top of that, the presence of the following two processes must be checked:

- `rabbitmq-server`: This is obvious but should not be forgotten!
- **epmd**: The Erlang Port Mapper Daemon plays a critical role in the clustering mechanism and, as such, should be carefully monitored.

Finally, the occurrence of ERROR REPORT entries in the main RabbitMQ logfile needs to be monitored as well. This logfile is typically located at: `/var/log/rabbitmq/rabbit@<hostname>.log`.

You now have the means to gather a holistic view of your RabbitMQ brokers all across your network in order to be proactive and stay on top of issues before they become too problematic.

Summary

In this chapter, you learned how RabbitMQ delivers powerful features, such as clustering or federation, in an elegant and easy-to-grasp manner. Using these features, you increased the availability and overall resilience of your messaging infrastructure. You also learned how to keep an eye on these brokers and be alerted if anything goes wrong with one of your RabbitMQ instances.

In the next and final chapter of this book, you'll learn about testing and tracing strategies that will allow you to develop and maintain applications in the long run.

8
Testing and Tracing Applications

Testing is essential to software engineering; no application can gracefully evolve over time if it is not associated with a consummate set of automated tests that act as a safety net against regression. Indeed, beyond validating that applications exhibit the intended behavior, testing is about defeating the test of time. RabbitMQ applications do not escape this rule, as this chapter explains in detail. Sometimes, reflecting about the code and testing it is not enough. Tracing comes into play when an actual application is executed and its inputs/outputs are scrutinized in order to get a deeper understanding of what it does. This chapter presents two handy tracing tools provided by RabbitMQ, which are very likely to become prominent in your developer's toolbox.

In this chapter, you will learn about the tools and techniques to do the following:

- Unit testing RabbitMQ applications
- Writing integration tests for these applications
- Tracing the AMQP protocol
- Tracing the RabbitMQ broker

Testing RabbitMQ applications

Developers at Clever Coney Media are test infected; they can't ship any piece of software that hasn't been properly tested in an automated fashion and with enough coverage. So how is it that you haven't seen any test until now? We wanted to keep the main focus on RabbitMQ and AMQP, so we didn't include testing in the discussions. As we're closing this book, now is a good time to revisit the code you've written and detail the tests that were created for it. We will focus on the main Java application, as it is where the vast majority of the critical code resides; however, the principles and practices you will learn about are applicable to any language or platform.

Your approach to test RabbitMQ applications is twofold:

- Create a set of unit tests that exercise the behavior of your classes, one by one and in isolation. In these unit tests, use mock objects instead of the actual RabbitMQ client classes to ensure that things are wired up together the way they should. Leverage these mock objects to test failure scenarios by raising exceptions.

- Create a set of integration tests that exercise your classes as a whole and run them against a live instance of RabbitMQ. Mock-driven testing is indeed no guarantee that things will work as intended in the real world, hence the necessity to test code with an actual broker.

Let's start unit testing your code.

Unit testing RabbitMQ applications

You've settled on **Mockito** (http://mockito.org) as your mocking framework of choice, because it's able to mock both interfaces and concrete classes (the RabbitMQ client contains both), ties perfectly with **JUnit**, has an awesome syntax, and "Does The Right Thing™" by default! Because Mockito works great with JUnit, you'll be able to run these unit tests as part of your Maven build using the standard **Surefire** plug-in (http://maven.apache.org/surefire/maven-surefire-plugin/).

[Mocha is a good mocking framework that you could use to test the Ruby code (http://gofreerange.com/mocha/docs/).]

Let's focus on unit testing the `RabbitMqManager` class, as it's the foremost class of the Java application. You first need to create the test class and initialize the **SUT (System Under Test)**. This is how you do it:

```
@RunWith(MockitoJUnitRunner.class)
public class RabbitMqManagerTest
```

```
{
     private static final Address[] TEST_ADDRESSES = {new
Address("fake")};

     @Mock
     private ConnectionFactory connectionFactory;

     @Mock
     private Connection connection;

     @Mock
     private Channel channel;

     private RabbitMqManager rabbitMqManager;

     @Before
     public void initialize() throws Exception
     {
          rabbitMqManager = new RabbitMqManager(connectionFactory, TEST_
ADDRESSES);
          when(connection.getAddress()).thenReturn(InetAddress.
getLocalHost());
     }
```

As you can see, you declared mocks for the principal classes that are involved when dealing with RabbitMQ: `connectionFactory`, `connection`, and `channel`. Then you initialize the `RabbitMQManager` class with the array that contains a fake address. It's fine, because no actual connection attempt will be made since we're mocking the RabbitMQ classes. You may wonder whether you should have several addresses there in order to test the connection fall-back mechanism onto which the cluster client relies. The answer is no; this is a behavior provided by the actual RabbitMQ client library and not by any of your code.

 Trust that the libraries you use are tested and do not retest them.

You've also attached a global behavior to the `getAddress()` method of the `connection` mock, so it returns a valid `InetAddress` instance, which spares you from doing it again and again in all the tests. Let's now detail a few tests that you've written to exercise the `start()` method:

```
@Test
public void startFailure() throws Exception
```

```
    {
        when(connectionFactory.newConnection(TEST_ADDRESSES))
            .thenThrow( new RuntimeException("simulated failure"));

        rabbitMqManager.start();

        final List<Runnable> scheduleReconnection = rabbitMqManager.
    getExecutor().shutdownNow();

        assertThat(scheduleReconnection.size(), is(1));
    }
```

In this test, you've first configured the `connectionFactory` mock to throw an exception when asked to create a new connection. This will simulate an issue when communicating with RabbitMQ. Note that you're throwing `RuntimeException` and not `IOException`, which is the checked exception that is thrown by `newConnection()`. This is because you want to ensure that your code can actually handle any exception that could bubble up through this method call, which is its intended behavior. You've also made it clear in the exception message that it is an intentional one.

[Always make your test exception messages explicit, so they can't be confused with actual exceptions.]

After that, you actually call the `start()` method, which is the main purpose of this test. If you remember its behavior from *Chapter 2, Creating an Application Inbox*, the `start()` method should have scheduled a reconnection task in case of a connection failure. That's why you shut down the executor encapsulated by the `RabbitMqManager` class and assert that it actually contained a scheduled `Runnable` instance. At this point, you're happy with this first test and move on to testing a successful start attempt as follows:

```
@Test
public void startSuccess() throws Exception
{
    when(connectionFactory.newConnection(TEST_ADDRESSES))
        .thenReturn(connection);

    rabbitMqManager.start();

    verify(connection).addShutdownListener(rabbitMqManager);
}
```

This test is short and sweet: the `connectionFactory` mock is configured to return the `connection` mock. The only assertion you've added is a verification of the fact that `RabbitMqManager` has registered itself as a shutdown listener on the `connection` mock. This is enough to ensure that the expected behavior kicks in when a connection is successfully created. Finally, you add another test to verify that the actual reconnection mechanism works as follows:

```
@Test
public void startFailureThenSuccess() throws Exception
{

    when(connectionFactory.newConnection(TEST_ADDRESSES))
        .thenThrow( new RuntimeException("simulated connection
            failure"))
        .thenReturn(connection);

    rabbitMqManager.setReconnectDelaySeconds(0);

    rabbitMqManager.start();

    Thread.sleep(100L);

    verify(connectionFactory, times(2))
        .newConnection(TEST_ADDRESSES);
    verify(connection).addShutdownListener(rabbitMqManager);
    verifyNoMoreInteractions(connectionFactory);
}
```

Let's detail the notable bits in this test. First, you configured the `connectionFactory` mock to initially fail then succeed when asked to create a new connection. Then you set the reconnection delay to be `0` so that `RabbitMqManager` retries right away. After starting it, you ponder for a few milliseconds before asserting that everything went fine. It's a little unfortunate that `Thread.sleep` has to be used, but there is no testing seam that we could use to register a synchronization primitive to block the testing thread just at the needed time.

 Avoid sleeping tests as much as possible; they slow down your tests and can exhibit erratic behaviors in a slow or busy continuous integration server.

The verifications in this test ensure that the `newConnection` method has been called twice, that the `RabbitMqManager` class has registered itself as a shutdown listener (as it should in case of connection success), and that no other interaction has occurred with `connectionFactory` (as expected after a connection success).

Many other tests are needed in order to exercise the channel creation and closure and the subscription management features of `RabbitMqManager`, but we will just detail one extra test. The following is what you've written to test a successful execution of a `ChannelCallable` instance via the `call` method:

```
@Test
public void callSuccess() throws Exception
{
    when(channel.isOpen()).thenReturn(true);
    when(connection.createChannel()).thenReturn(channel);
    rabbitMqManager.setConnection(connection);

    final Channel expectedChannel = channel;

    final String result = rabbitMqManager.call(new
ChannelCallable<String>()
    {
        @Override
        public String getDescription()
        {
            return "success";
        }

        @Override
        public String call(final Channel channel) throws IOException
        {
            return channel == expectedChannel ? "ok" : "bad";
        }
    });

    assertThat(result, is("ok"));

    verify(channel).close();
}
```

Let's detail this test bit by bit as follows:

- You've configured the `channel` mock to act as if it's open and the `connection` mock to return the `channel` mock when asked for a new channel. This will ensure that the `call` method effectively creates a new channel.

- You've also configured `RabbitMqManager` with the `connection` mock; this way, you do not need to call the `start` method to establish a connection. This is important to contain the test to only exercise the logic you're interested in.

- The copy of `channel` to the final variable `expectedChannel` is a Java technicality; it's necessary to allow using it inside the `ChannelCallable` anonymous inner class that follows.

- The `ChannelCallable` class itself ensures that `expectedChannel` has been passed to it by the `RabbitMqManager` class and confirms it by returning `ok` to the caller.

- The assertions of the test consist in checking that `ok` has been returned and `close()` has been called on `channel`, which is the last thing the `call` method should do after executing `ChannelCallable`.

With this approach, you've been able to achieve almost 100 percent test coverage for your classes using the RabbitMQ client SDK. This is a great position to be in as it will ensure that any breaking change will be caught at development time. This said, you also want to add tests that will exercise your code against a real broker instead of using mocks. It's time to write some integration tests.

Integration testing RabbitMQ applications

Unlike what you've just done with unit tests, which are aware of all the internals of the tested application, integration tests focus on testing a system as a whole. They are sometimes referred to as black-box testing, which is opposite to white-box or clear-box testing. Your goal with integration testing your RabbitMQ application is to gain confidence that not only are things wired up internally as they should be, but also that they really work as intended.

> Integration tests should be automated and reproducible. They should not require any manual configuration, so they can be run as often as necessary without being a hurdle for developers. Like boy scouts, they should clean up after themselves so that they don't mess the environment they're running in. This is essential if they're intended to run on production systems.

You will use JUnit to run the integration tests so that they're developed in a familiar fashion, are automated, and can easily be run from a programming environment. You will also use the **Failsafe** Maven plugin (`https://maven.apache.org/surefire/maven-failsafe-plugin/`) to run these tests as part of your Maven build, but only as part of a specific profile. Indeed, you do not want these tests to run by default; otherwise, the build may fail when run on a machine where RabbitMQ is not running (like your continuous integration server).

Let's look in detail at the test that validates that the subscription mechanism works well. First, you need to create and configure the SUT, which is again an instance of RabbitMqManager, but this time configured to connect to a live RabbitMQ broker as follows:

```
public class RabbitMqManagerIT
{
    private RabbitMqManager rabbitMqManager;

    @Before
    public void configureAndStart() throws Exception
    {
        final ConnectionFactory connectionFactory = new
ConnectionFactory();
        connectionFactory.setUsername(System.getProperty("test.rmq.
username", "ccm-dev"));
        connectionFactory.setPassword(System.getProperty("test.rmq.
password", "coney123"));
        connectionFactory.setVirtualHost(System.getProperty("test.rmq.
vhost", "ccm-dev-vhost"));

        final String addresses = System.getProperty("test.rmq.
addresses", "localhost:5672");

        rabbitMqManager = new RabbitMqManager(connectionFactory,
Address.parseAddresses(addresses));

        System.out.printf("%nRunning integration tests on %s%n%n",
addresses);

        rabbitMqManager.start();
    }

    @After
    public void stop() throws Exception
    {
        rabbitMqManager.stop();
    }
```

As you can see, before reaching the point where RabbitMqManager gets instantiated, we extract configuration values from system properties, falling back to default values that point to a locally running RabbitMQ broker. This approach allows you to point the tests at any broker by simply providing different connection parameters to the test.

Integration tests make great smoke tests. Make them easily reusable so that you can run them against any system to quickly validate that they are working fine.

Now let's look at the test itself. It's pretty long, so before delving into the code, let's talk about what it will do. You want to test if the subscription mechanism works. For this, you will: create a test queue, subscribe to it, send a message to it, and finally assert that the message has been consumed by the subscriber. With this said, let's look at the first part of the test, which takes care of setting the test queue as follows:

```
@Test
public void subscriptionTest() throws Exception
{
    final String queue = rabbitMqManager.call(new
ChannelCallable<String>()
    {
        @Override
        public String getDescription()
        {
            return "subscription test setup";
        }

        @Override
        public String call(final Channel channel)
          throws IOException
        {
            final DeclareOk declareOk = channel.queueDeclare("",
              false, true, true, null);
            return declareOk.getQueue();
        }
    });
```

The important bit here is that you create an automatically named, exclusive, nondurable, and auto-delete queue. Why these options? You want the queue name to be unique so that there is no possible collision if another developer runs the test on the same broker. For further protection from any risk of having another consumer interacting with this queue, you made it exclusive. Finally, you do not want either the messages or the queue itself to be retained when you're done with the test, hence the nondurability and autodeletion attributes. Next, we create the subscription as follows:

```
final AtomicReference<byte[]> delivered = new
AtomicReference<byte[]>();
final CountDownLatch latch = new CountDownLatch(1);
```

```
final Subscription subscription = rabbitMqManager.
createSubscription(queue,
    new SubscriptionDeliverHandler()
    {
        @Override
        public void handleDelivery(final Channel channel,
            final Envelope envelope,
            final BasicProperties properties,
            final byte[] body)
        {
            delivered.set(body);
            latch.countDown();
        }
    });

    assertThat(subscription.getChannel().isOpen(), is(true));
```

This bit is very interesting because here you can use synchronization primitives instead of having to resort to a `sleep` statement as you did before. Indeed, the latch will allow you to block the test thread until the `handleDelivery` method has been called and the message body value set on the `delivered` atomic reference. Without this mechanism, there would be no way to check what message was delivered or when it was delivered, since it is done by a thread other than the testing thread. That said, you can right away assert that the subscription encapsulates an open channel. With this in place, it's now time to send a test message to the queue as follows:

```
final byte[] body = rabbitMqManager.call(new ChannelCallable<byte[]>()
{
    @Override
    public String getDescription()
    {
        return "publish test message";
    }

    @Override
    public byte[] call(final Channel channel) throws IOException
    {
        final byte[] body = UUID.randomUUID().toString().getBytes();
        channel.basicPublish("", queue, null, body);
        return body;
    }
});
```

Nothing particularly novel here. You may wonder why we are creating a random body payload for the test message. This is to ensure that the test will be consuming the right message and not a message that could be lingering from a previous test. Notice that you have to target the default exchange to be able to send to the test queue directly, which frees you from the need to declare a test exchange and bind the queue to it.

> If you're concerned that test messages could be mixed with real ones in a tested broker, add a custom flag to the messages' headers to tag them as ignorable.

The following final code fragment is where the assertions happen:

```
if (!latch.await(1, TimeUnit.MINUTES))
{
    fail("Handler not called on time");
}

assertThat(delivered.get(), is(body));

subscription.stop();
assertThat(subscription.getChannel(), is(nullValue()));
```

Did you see how you've leveraged `latch` to block the test thread until the message gets delivered? Nothing should ever be blocked forever, so you've been wise enough to cap the waiting period to one minute and fail the test if no message has been received after that.

At this point, you've covered your bases in term of testing. You're now pretty confident that any regression will be caught at an early stage thanks to the barrage of unit and integration tests you've created.

> Our focus is on testing RabbitMQ-related code exclusively; however, to be thorough, you will add an extra layer of integration tests that will exercise the application as a whole via **HTTP** and **WebSockets** interactions.

When adding new features, it's sometimes convenient to step-debug into an application to trace its execution. The next section will detail how to achieve this with RabbitMQ.

Tracing RabbitMQ

Tracing the execution of a program is a convenient way to figure out what is really happening under the hood when reasoning about a particular behavior leads to no firm conclusion. Usually, the buck stops at the border where the application interacts with external resources such as the RabbitMQ broker. The good news is that RabbitMQ provides two tools that can be of tremendous help when it comes to tracing the interactions with a broker.

The first of these tools is **Tracer**, an AMQP-aware network proxy that can be placed between a RabbitMQ client and a broker in order to gain insight into the interactions that are happening between each other. Tracer is available as part of the Java client download available at `http://www.rabbitmq.com/download.html`.

 The complete documentation for Tracer and **PerfTest** (a basic load test tool) can be found at `http://www.rabbitmq.com/java-tools.html`.

After installation, Tracer can be started with the following:

```
runjava.sh com.rabbitmq.tools.Tracer [listenPort] [connectHost]
    [connectPort].
```

All the parameters are optional. If left blank, Tracer will start a local proxy listening on port `5673` and connect to a local RabbitMQ on port `5672`. Since you're happy with the defaults, you start Tracer with just the following command line:

```
$ ./runjava.sh com.rabbitmq.tools.Tracer
```

Now you can run the integration tests you've just created through this proxy. Do you remember that we made the connection information configurable on these tests? The approach is going to pay off now as we will configure them to go through the proxy port instead of directly hitting the RabbitMQ broker. You do this by running the following command line:

```
$ mvn -Pintegration_tests -Dtest.rmq.addresses=localhost:5673 verify
```

The output of Tracer is very verbose as it includes the complete details of the AMQP operations. Hereafter only the columns that show the channel ID, interaction direct (`->` is client to broker and `<-` is opposite), and the name of the operation is reproduced, with the interactions related to the subscriber highlighted:

```
    ch#0 <- <connection.start>
    ch#0 -> <connection.start-ok>
    ch#0 <- <connection.tune>
    ch#0 -> <connection.tune-ok>
```

```
ch#0 -> <connection.open>
ch#0 <- <connection.open-ok>
ch#1 -> <channel.open>
ch#1 <- <channel.open-ok>
ch#1 -> <queue.declare>
ch#1 <- <queue.declare-ok>
ch#1 -> <channel.close>
ch#1 <- <channel.close-ok>()
ch#1 -> <channel.open>
ch#1 <- <channel.open-ok>
ch#1 -> <basic.consume>
ch#1 <- <basic.consume-ok>
ch#2 -> <channel.open>
ch#2 <- <channel.open-ok>
ch#2 -> <basic.publish>
ch#2 -> <channel.close>
ch#1 <- <basic.deliver>
ch#2 <- <channel.close-ok>
ch#1 -> <basic.cancel>
ch#1 <- <basic.cancel-ok>
ch#1 -> <channel.close>
ch#1 <- <channel.close-ok>
ch#0 -> <connection.close>
ch#0 <- <connection.close-ok>
```

You can see the operations from the client and the responses from the broker, typically being named after the operation and suffixed with -ok. In essence, the following is the AMQP synopsis of the test code you're running:

- Establish a connection
- Open a channel, use it to declare the test queue, and close it
- Open a channel, use it to consume a queue
- Open a channel, use it to publish the test message, and close it
- Receive the message delivery, cancel the consumer, and close its channel
- Close the connection

Notice how the connection start and tune operations are initiated by the broker as a response to establishing the connection to it. Also, notice that the channel number gets reused after being closed; it may seem that the same channel #1 has been used for creating the test queue and subscribing to it, but that's not the case since this channel has been explicitly closed. Only its identifier has been reused.

The Tracer may report bogus uncaught `java.io.EOFException` exceptions; this is a known and benign issue. You can confirm in the RabbitMQ log that no communication error actually happened.

Tracer is a very powerful tool to easily gain a deep understanding of the AMQP protocol and the usage your applications make of it. However, it requires you to insert a proxy between a client and the broker it connects to. Fear not if this is an issue; RabbitMQ has more than one trick in its bag of tracing tools.

Drinking at the Firehose

RabbitMQ offers the possibility of spying on all message publications and delivery operations that happens in a particular virtual host of a broker. This feature is called the **Firehose** tracer. When activated on a virtual host, a copy of all published and all delivered messages is sent to the `amq.rabbitmq.trace` exchange (which is automatically created in every virtual host).

The routing key used for messages published to the `amq.rabbitmq.trace` exchange is `publish.<exchange_name>` for publication events and `deliver.<queue_name>` for message deliveries. The original message body is carried to the copies sent to this exchange. Extra information about the original publication or delivery event are added in a set of headers, including `exchange_name` for the name of the exchange where the message was originally published or redelivered if the message has been delivered more than once.

The complete reference guide of the Firehose tracer can be found at `http://www.rabbitmq.com/firehose.html`.

You want to use the Firehose when running the integration tests to see the exchanged messages from the broker's standpoint. Before activating the Firehose on RabbitMQ, you need first to create a client application that will subscribe to the exchange and print out the messages that come to it. For this, you create the following Python script:

```
#!/usr/bin/env python
import amqp

connection = amqp.Connection(host='localhost', userid='ccm-dev',
password='coney123', virtual_host='ccm-dev-vhost')
channel = connection.channel()

EXCHANGE = 'amq.rabbitmq.trace'
```

```
QUEUE = 'firehose-queue'

channel.queue_declare(queue=QUEUE, durable=False, auto_delete=True,
exclusive=True)
channel.queue_bind(queue=QUEUE, exchange=EXCHANGE, routing_key='#')

def handle_message(message):
    print message.routing_key, '->', message.properties, message.body
    print '-----------------------------'

channel.basic_consume(callback=handle_message, queue=QUEUE, no_
ack=True)

print ' [*] Waiting for messages. To exit press CTRL+C'
while channel.callbacks:
    channel.wait()

channel.close()
connection.close()
```

This code should be very familiar; it is almost the same one that you used to log errors in *Chapter 4, Handling Application Logs*. The main difference is that this time you're using a transient queue bound to the `amq.rabbitmq.trace` exchange, which doesn't need to be re-declared since it is by design guaranteed to be present.

After starting this script, you turn the Firehose on by running the following command line:

```
$ sudo rabbitmqctl -p ccm-dev-vhost trace_on
Starting tracing for vhost "ccm-dev-vhost" ...
...done.
```

Now you can run the integration tests again, this time on the standard port since no proxying is needed with the Firehose:

```
$ mvn -Pintegration_tests verify
```

Let's now look at the following output of the Firehose consumer Python script:

```
publish. -> {'application_headers': {u'node': u'rabbit@pegasus',
u'exchange_name': u'', u'routing_keys': [u'amq.gen-vTMWL--
04lap8s8JPbX5gA'], u'properties': {}}} 93b56787-b4f5-41e1-8c6f-
d5f9b64275ca

-----------------------------
```

```
deliver.amq.gen-vTMWL--04lap8s8JPbX5gA -> {'application_headers':
{u'node': u'rabbit@pegasus', u'exchange_name': u'', u'redelivered': 0,
u'routing_keys': [u'amq.gen-vTMWL--04lap8s8JPbX5gA'], u'properties': {}}}
93b56787-b4f5-41e1-8c6f-d5f9b64275ca
```

As you can see, the publication to the default exchange (remember, its name is an empty string) and the delivery to the automatically named test queue are clearly visible. All the details that concern them are readily available in the message properties.

Keep in mind that running the Firehose is taxing for the RabbitMQ broker, so when you're done with your tracing session, shut it down with the following:

```
$ sudo rabbitmqctl -p ccm-dev-vhost trace_off

Stopping tracing for vhost "ccm-dev-vhost" ...

...done.
```

The Firehose will come handy when tracing what's happening between your different applications and your RabbitMQ brokers in depth. Keep in mind that using unique message IDs, as you've learned throughout this book, will help you a lot when the time comes to perform forensics analysis and trace the progression of messages across your complete infrastructure.

Summary

In this chapter, you learned about unit and integration testing RabbitMQ applications, thus increasing your confidence and capacity to refactor and helping you maintain them in the long run. You've also discovered two powerful tracing tools to peek deeper under the hood of the AMQP protocol and the RabbitMQ broker.

Armed with this knowledge and everything else you learned throughout this book, you're now fully equipped to build production-grade distributed RabbitMQ applications that will scale and last.

RabbitMQ is a solid, stable, and dependable messaging broker. Now go and build something great with it.

Message Schemas

This appendix contains the different message schemas used by Clever Coney Media to specify the JSON representations of the messages they send through RabbitMQ.

 Messages are represented using the JSON format, `http://json.org/`. Their definitions are expressed using draft 3 of the JSON schema language, `http://tools.ietf.org/html/draft-zyp-json-schema-03`. (CCM doesn't use draft 4 because their code generation tool doesn't support it yet.)

User message

The user message schema is used to represent all user messages (user-to-user, topic, or public-announce messages), and is coded as follows:

```
{
    "$schema": "http://json-schema.org/draft-03/schema#",
    "$content_type": "application/vnd.ccm.pmsg.v1+json",
    "type": "object",
    "additionalProperties": false,
    "properties": {
        "time_sent": {
            "type":"string",
            "format":"utc-millisec"
        },
        "sender_id": {
            "type": "integer",
            "optional": "false"
        },
        "addressee_id": {
```

```
                    "type": "integer",
                    "optional": "true"
                },
                "topic": {
                    "type": "string",
                    "optional": "true"
                },
                "subject": {
                    "type": "string",
                    "optional": "false"
                },
                "content": {
                    "type": "string",
                    "optional": "false"
                }
            }
        }
    }
```

Authentication messages

The following schemas represent the request and response messages used by the
authentication service.

Login

The authentication service exposes a login operation. The following pair of schemas
defines the request and response messages it deals with.

Request

The request schema represents a login request message that allows us to validate a
user's credentials, and is coded as follows:

```
    {
        "$schema": "http://json-schema.org/draft-03/schema#",
        "$content_type": "application/vnd.ccm.login.req.v1+json",
        "type": "object",
        "additionalProperties": false,
        "properties": {
            "username": {
                "type":"string",
                "required": true
```

```
            },
            "password": {
                "type":"string",
                "required": true
            }
        }
    }
```

Response

The response schema represents the response to a login request, including a token that can be used to perform authenticated operations, and is coded as follows:

```
{
    "$schema": "http://json-schema.org/draft-03/schema#",
    "$content_type": "application/vnd.ccm.login.res.v1+json",
    "type": "object",
    "additionalProperties": false,
    "properties": {
        "success": {
            "type":"boolean",
            "required": true
        },
        "authentication_token": {
            "type":"string",
            "required": true
        }
    }
}
```

Logout

Another operation exposed by the authentication service is logout. The following two schemas represent the request and response messages the logout operation works with.

Request

A logout request message is defined by the following schema:

```
{
    "$schema": "http://json-schema.org/draft-03/schema#",
    "$content_type": "application/vnd.ccm.logout.req.v1+json",
    "type": "object",
    "additionalProperties": false,
    "properties": {
        "authentication_token": {
            "type":"string",
            "required": true
        }
    }
}
```

Response

The following schema represents the response after a logout operation has been attempted:

```
{
    "$schema": "http://json-schema.org/draft-03/schema#",
    "$content_type": "application/vnd.ccm.logout.res.v1+json",
    "type": "object",
    "additionalProperties": false,
    "properties": {
        "success": {
            "type":"boolean",
            "required": true
        }
    }
}
```

Generic error message

Whenever something goes wrong when a service processes a request message, it can return an error message to provide information about the failure. The following schema represents such a generic error message that can be returned not only by the authentication service, but by any service CCM will create:

```
{
    "$schema": "http://json-schema.org/draft-03/schema#",
    "$content_type": "application/vnd.ccm.error.v1+json",
```

```
        "type": "object",
        "additionalProperties": false,
        "properties": {
            "context": {
                "type":"string",
                "required": true
            },
            "message": {
                "type":"string",
                "required": true
            }
        }
    }
}
```

Index

respond method 111
Rich Internet Application (RIA) 13, 24
routing key 31, 92

S

security cookie 118
sendUserMessage class 38
server-push approach 50
Service-oriented Architecture (SOA) 101
service-oriented messaging
  about 101, 102
  queues, replying to 102-105
  service requests, routing 105
severity.facility 72
shovel plugin 127
shutdownCompleted method 26, 27
Simple Mail Transfer Protocol. *See* SMTP
single point of failure (SPOF) 117
SMTP 9
socket descriptors 136
Spring AMQP
  URL 25
start method 26
start() method 141, 142
stop method 56
store_log_data function 74, 75
sudo rabbitmqctl set_policy command 88
Surefire plugin
  URL 140
SUT (System Under Test) 140

T

testing 139
time 92
topic! 43
topic messages
  adding 43-46
toString method 56
Tracer 150, 152

U

unit testing
  RabbitMQ applications 140-145
upstreams 129
user-fanout exchange 67
user messages
  fetching 39, 40
  sending 35, 37
user message schema 155
UserMessageServerEndpoint 58
users
  configuring 19, 21, 22

V

vhost 21

W

WebSocket
  about 50
  endpoint, typing into 58-61
  URL 50
WebSocket endpoint
  typing into 58-61

Z

ZeroMQ. *See* ØMQ

Thank you for buying
RabbitMQ Essentials

About Packt Publishing

Packt, pronounced 'packed', published its first book "*Mastering phpMyAdmin for Effective MySQL Management*" in April 2004 and subsequently continued to specialize in publishing highly focused books on specific technologies and solutions.

Our books and publications share the experiences of your fellow IT professionals in adapting and customizing today's systems, applications, and frameworks. Our solution based books give you the knowledge and power to customize the software and technologies you're using to get the job done. Packt books are more specific and less general than the IT books you have seen in the past. Our unique business model allows us to bring you more focused information, giving you more of what you need to know, and less of what you don't.

Packt is a modern, yet unique publishing company, which focuses on producing quality, cutting-edge books for communities of developers, administrators, and newbies alike. For more information, please visit our website: www.packtpub.com.

About Packt Open Source

In 2010, Packt launched two new brands, Packt Open Source and Packt Enterprise, in order to continue its focus on specialization. This book is part of the Packt Open Source brand, home to books published on software built around Open Source licences, and offering information to anybody from advanced developers to budding web designers. The Open Source brand also runs Packt's Open Source Royalty Scheme, by which Packt gives a royalty to each Open Source project about whose software a book is sold.

Writing for Packt

We welcome all inquiries from people who are interested in authoring. Book proposals should be sent to author@packtpub.com. If your book idea is still at an early stage and you would like to discuss it first before writing a formal book proposal, contact us; one of our commissioning editors will get in touch with you.

We're not just looking for published authors; if you have strong technical skills but no writing experience, our experienced editors can help you develop a writing career, or simply get some additional reward for your expertise.

RabbitMQ Cookbook

ISBN: 978-1-84951-650-1   Paperback: 288 pages

Over 70 practical recipes to help you develop messaging applications using RabbitMQ with the help of plenty of real-life examples

1. Create scalable distributed applications with RabbitMQ.

2. Exploit RabbitMQ on both web and mobile platforms.

3. Deploy message services on cloud computing platforms.

RabbitMQ Messaging Application Development How-to [Instant]

ISBN: 978-1-78216-574-3   Paperback: 54 pages

Build scalable message-based applications with RabbitMQ

1. Learn something new in an Instant! A short, fast, focused guide delivering immediate results.

2. Learn how to build message-based applications with RabbitMQ using a practical Node.js e-commerce example.

3. Implement various messaging patterns including asynchronous work queues, publish subscribe and topics.

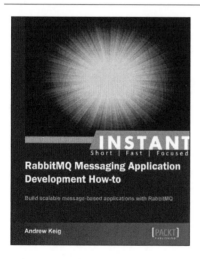

Apache CloudStack Cloud Computing

ISBN: 978-1-78216-010-6   Paperback: 294 pages

Leverage the power of CloudStack and learn to extend the CloudStack environment

1. Install, deploy, and manage a cloud service using CloudStack.

2. Step-by-step instructions on setting up and running the leading open source cloud platform CloudStack.

3. Set up an IaaS cloud environment using CloudStack.

OpenStack Cloud Computing Cookbook *Second Edition*

ISBN: 978-1-78216-758-7   Paperback: 396 pages

Over 100 recipes to successfully set up and manage your OpenStack cloud environments with complete coverage of Nova, Swift, Keystone, Glance, Horizon, Neutron, and Cinder

1. Updated for OpenStack Grizzly.

2. Learn how to install, configure, and manage all of the OpenStack core projects including new topics such as block storage and software defined networking.

3. Learn how to build your Private Cloud utilizing DevOps and Continuous Integration tools and techniques.

Please check **www.PacktPub.com** for information on our titles

12611389R00102

Printed in Great Britain
by Amazon.co.uk, Ltd.,
Marston Gate.